BENINGFIELD'S
VANISHING SONGBIRDS

BENINGFIELD'S VANISHING SONGBIRDS

Text by Betty Beningfield
Introduction by Robin Page

BIRD'S FARM BOOKS

Published by Bird's Farm Books, Barton, Cambridgeshire CB3 7AG
www.crtbarton.com
Distributed by Merlin Unwin Books, 7 Corve Street, Ludlow, Shropshire

ISBN 0 905232 19 4

Designed by Jim Reader
Design and production in association with Book Production Consultants plc,
25–27 High Street, Chesterton, Cambridge CB4 1ND
www.bpccam.co.uk

Printed and bound in Great Britain by The Burlington Press, Foxton, Cambridge

ENDPAPERS: *The restored landscape of the Countryside Restoration Trust's Lark Rise Farm.*
FRONTISPIECE: *Two important songbirds of the garden, the blackbird and the song thrush.*

Contents

Acknowledgements

There are many people whose help has been invaluable in preparing this tribute to the life and work of Gordon Beningfield. Some have allowed pictures to be photographed, others have been available with advice and reminiscences and some have supplied photographs and transparencies.

They include: Terry Andrewartha, Martin Smith, Nigel Housden, Ian Cameron and Jill Hollis of Cameron Books, Colin Carr, Dena and Terry Duncan, Jill and Roy Marriott, Mr and Mrs Boating, Mr Tom Dean, Mr Steve Dean, Mrs Jenny Tingle, Richard Mabey, Brian Sawford, Mr Paul Seabrook, Betty and Frank Brazier, Mr and Mrs John Hawker, Mrs Nicola Hereghon, Vivienne Schuster, Professor W. Hill, Alistair McGregor, Bronwen Boyce and Sally and Sarah Beningfield. Thanks too are due to Jim Reader and Franca Holden of Book Production Consultants.

Almost certainly I have forgotten some names – but I am grateful to everybody who has helped ensure the publication of *Beningfield's Vanishing Songbirds*.

R. P.

Introduction

Beningfield's Vanishing Songbirds is the book that Gordon Beningfield, the artist, was working on at the time of his tragic and untimely death. With the invaluable help and support of his widow Betty, we have searched out paintings and finished the book as a tribute to a very special artist and a true guardian of the countryside.

Throughout the book we have quoted the poetry and prose of John Clare, which Gordon loved. Clare's grammatical expertise was about as good as mine and so most of his spelling and lack of punctuation have been left as he produced it.

All the royalties from this book will be going to Betty Beningfield and in addition I will be making a donation on every book sold to the Gordon Beningfield Memorial Appeal. I have published this book on behalf of the Countryside Restoration Trust in the hope that the Appeal Fund will benefit significantly as a direct result.

The main aim of the Appeal is to buy a Dorset farm in memory of Gordon as he loved the county and its association with wildlife, farming and the works of Thomas Hardy. Donations should be sent to 'The Gordon Beningfield Memorial Appeal', c/o The Countryside Restoration Trust, Barton, Cambs CB3 7AG.

ROBIN PAGE

Foreword

Gordon Beningfield was probably the most gifted countryside artist of his generation and he was also one of the most prolific. His watercolour paintings of butterflies, birds, farms and the general countryside had a detail and an interpretation that made them quite exceptional. His paintings were not completed simply to fulfil a commission or to promote his name; Gordon was an active campaigner for conservation and the countryside and he saw each painting he produced as another arrow fired to defend the things he loved.

Unlike so many writers, artists, broadcasters and 'celebrities' he was not prepared to sit on the fence for the sake of a sale or another television appearance; he said what he thought and he said it with passion and eloquence.

For many years, at the end of each project, Gordon would say: 'I am going to slow down now: I want more time to watch butterflies, hear the birds sing and paint in my time, as I did when I started, rather than slave away simply to meet deadlines.' It was a vain hope, for as soon as one project ended, he saw another battle to be fought with paint-brush and pen, or another point to make – and off he went again in top gear.

So it was with *Beningfield's Vanishing Songbirds*. Despondent at the continuing industrialisation of farming through the Common Agriculture Policy, desperate to fight for the birds he loved, but which were continuing to disappear – the skylark, the lapwing and the swallow – and angry at what he saw as the cynical attacks on the countryside and country people by urban- and suburban-minded politicians, he threw himself into the new project before he had even been commissioned to do so.

For Betty, his childhood sweetheart turned wife, his daughters Sally and Sarah, and for his friends it was a hard time. No sooner had he started the book than his cancer returned, after several years of productive remission. His first visit to the clinic coincided with the Countryside Rally in Hyde Park, London on 1 July 1997. He arrived at Hyde Park as the crowd was dispersing – 125,000 country people making a point. Gordon was so disappointed to have missed it. He did not hunt, had given up shooting and the River Gade had dried up so that he could not fly fish, but he regarded country sports as important parts of both conservation and rural culture and he wanted to be in the fight to protect them. After all, many of his own friends hunted, whether on horseback or rusty bikes, and his daughters had ridden with the Aldenham Harriers as teenagers.

He regarded the fight as far more than country sports; he believed that it was a battle for the whole countryside and he has since been proved right. He was anxious about farming, rural communities, vanishing wildlife, the lack of houses for village people, and the disappearance of village policemen, post offices, pubs and churches. He saw all these as part of the same fight and he viewed our present generation of urban-dominated politicians with contempt.

By the time of the Countryside March on 1 March 1998, when up to half a million country people and their friends marched through London, Gordon was confined to a hospital bed, much to his great frustration. He died on a beautiful spring morning on 4 May 1998. His family lost a husband and a father, I lost my closest friend and thousands of people lost a man that they admired and could identify with, for Gordon had the common touch and people loved him for it. By coincidence I lost my faithful little lurcher Bramble, exactly one year later and I remember him through one of Gordon's paintings.

I decided soon afterwards that *Beningfield's Vanishing Songbirds* must be finished as a tribute to an outstanding artist and conservationist. It has taken over three years to collect Gordon's paintings and put the book together. Betty has been very helpful during this

My faithful little lurcher Bramble,
painted for my fiftieth birthday.

Orange tip butterfly on a cuckoo flower.

time, as have many of Gordon's friends and so I hope the book is a fitting tribute to his talent.

I am aware that if Gordon had finished the book himself he would have painted far more 'vanishing' songbirds. He would have painted the willow warbler, the starling, the garden warbler, the turtle dove, the swallow, swift and house martin, and many more. But we have searched high and low and we have found paintings originally commissioned for earlier books and private individuals, which have enabled us to finish the book that he started so enthusiastically and passionately. It shows Gordon's versatility as an artist and I hope too that with Betty's tremendous help, Gordon's message has come over loud and clear. His view was simple: that we are still damaging our wildlife through greed, ignorance and indifference. His message would have been double-sided because he also believed that the destruction could be halted and that the richness and diversity of the countryside could be restored.

I had hoped to link this book with a television programme

about Gordon's life and work, as he did several television series for the BBC as well as a feature film, but sadly, as I expected, the Controller of BBC 2 turned it down. In the shallow world of glitz and celebrity that makes up so much of today's media trash, a gifted man like Gordon was evidently considered unsuitable for a forty minute programme on 'public service television'.

I became friendly with Gordon from the instant we met, well over twenty years ago. He came to interview me, for a BBC television programme, about my tame vixen, Rusty. We had much in common: we were both uneducated innocents in a very competitive and predominately urban world – he in painting and me with the pen. Our interests were almost identical except for one thing, I was embarrassingly ignorant about butterflies. Gordon was a self-taught expert whose expertise showed in his paintings, as he transformed butterfly 'illustration' into genuine art. His sheer enthusiasm pulled me into the world of butterflies: 'There's an orange tip (his favourite butterfly). Let's look for its eggs on the cuckoo flower'; and there they were.

Despite being associated with the countryside, in fact Gordon was born near the Pool of London on 31 October 1936, where his father worked as a lighterman. He remembered vividly the sights and sounds of the Blitz, which helped to develop a life-long love affair with the Spitfire. Despite moving with the family to Hertfordshire in 1941, Gordon maintained an emotional attachment to London and felt greatly honoured to receive the Freedom of the City of London in 1993. He also believed that if it was not for the mischief of politicians there would be no town/country divide.

At London Colney, in Hertfordshire, he went to the village Junior School and then the local Secondary Modern. He loved his late-starting country childhood, being enthralled by the wildlife he discovered around him and mixing with farmworkers, horse keepers, shepherds and gamekeepers.

Being dyslexic he found academic work difficult, but his teachers were quick to recognise his remarkable gift for drawing and painting. While his classmates concentrated on 'the Three R's', Gordon got on with his art. There were no bad feelings and Gordon maintained many of his childhood friendships for the rest of his life. He was President of the London Colney Old Boys Association, which also contained a high percentage of 'old girls', and each year they went on assorted trips on steam trains and buses.

He left school at fifteen; his choice of occupation was gamekeeping or painting. He chose the latter when offered an apprenticeship in ecclesiastical art with Faithcraft at St Albans, working on stained-glass windows, gold leaf and glass engraving. On moving to the company's London studio he walked by a Jaguar car every morning and vowed to buy his own one day. In recent years he owned a cosseted Jaguar, as well as two pre-World War II MGs. As an environmentalist he admitted the double standard, but admired the lines and engineering of all three vehicles which he regarded as technology meeting art.

After each week in London, he still roamed his beloved Hertfordshire countryside at weekends, sketching and painting the rich and varied wildlife. His technique was also helped by attending St Albans School of Art one day a week. After thirteen years of enjoying ecclesiastical work, he managed to accumulate so many private commissions for his watercolours that he left work to concentrate on his painting.

As his reputation grew, he was commissioned to produce some magnificent engraved glass windows for the Household Cavalry in the Guards Chapel, London. In the late 1970s and early 1980s his popularity jumped with a number of television series including 'In Deepest Britain' and 'In the Country'. 'Dorset Dream' explored his fascination with Hardy country and he became a self-taught expert on Thomas Hardy and a friend of Gertrude Bugler – who was cast by Hardy as Tess when the writer brought his novel to the stage.

A typical Beningfield landscape – quintessentially English – a blend of farm, field, wildlife and a wide sky.

Gordon believed that the wildlife and landscapes of Hardy could and should co-exist with modern farming methods and he would get depressed at the ravages caused by those farmers who turned their farms into production factories. He blamed the destruction of farmland wildlife on Europe's Common Agricultural Policy, and viewed such people as Edward Heath (the Prime Minister who took Britain into the European Economic Union) with complete contempt, regarding them as blind, eco-illiterate Europhiles.

His interest in butterflies developed partly through their capacity to indicate the health and diversity of the countryside. In 1978 he published his first book *Beningfield's Butterflies*. It greatly enhanced his reputation as he turned butterfly illustration into genuine art. In 1980 *Beningfield's Countryside* appeared, confirming both his talent and his popularity. It sold over 150,000 copies and was translated into five languages. Not bad for a dyslexic country boy who the army turned down for National Service! (This always amused Gordon: 'I would have loved to have gone in the army, but they thought I was too thick.')

In 1981 the Post Office commissioned him to design a set of butterfly postage stamps. These were so popular that in 1985 they were followed by a set of insects including the bumble bee and stag beetle. During the 1990s more books followed and in 1994 'This England' magazine awarded him its Silver Cross of St George for his work for the countryside. In 1997 the British Naturalists Association presented him with the Peter Scott Memorial Award.

But although Gordon was busy, gifted and dedicated, he was also a very funny and sociable man. Yes, he did get depressed about the state of politics and the countryside, but he was also excellent company and a reliable, loyal friend. Every year we would go the Shire Horse Show at Peterborough and Gordon and our mutual friend, the hyperactive, hedge-laying, antiquarian book-collecting 'Badger' Walker, would somehow arrive in the Press Tent for a bacon sandwich breakfast. At the Game Fair, Gordon would be immaculately dressed in his John Brocklehurst country clothing – the perfect gentleman; I would be in my jeans and trainers – the perfect peasant and Badger, the eccentric rustic, would be scurrying hither and thither making plastic bag caches of antiquarian books at every bookstand. Those were happy, laughter-filled days, visiting whatever stands took our fancy – John Brocklehurst, the RSPB, the Game Conservancy, the Countryside Alliance, ferret-keepers, stickmakers, gamekeepers and the purveyors of country wines. Whether duke or dustman, Gordon got on well with virtually everybody.

Out watching birds or looking for wild flowers he was the same: 'Look at the goldfinch, isn't it wonderful?' And then we would both see a bird and laugh before he had even said anything. Yes, it was a linnet, and out it would come: 'Look there's a bush with a linnet in-it; it's a linnet innit? Innit a linnet?'

Because of his skill at painting butterflies – here a Red Admiral on bind weed – Gordon was commissioned to paint a set of butterfly stamps for the Post Office in 1981.

An early Beningfield goldfinch already showing his skill at detail.

One of my funniest memories was when we were walking through one of our fields for BBC Radio's 'Woman's Hour'. We were wandering along a hedgerow describing what we saw. Gordon said: 'And here's a gatekeeper butterfly, it loves the bramble blossom on a sunny afternoon.' I heard a noise that sounded like a young kestrel and looking up said: 'And overhead we have a … … … PARROT.' Yes, it really was a parrot; where it came from and where it was going I have no idea. Gordon collapsed with uncontrollable laughter and sadly, we had to do the whole recording again.

I hope this book does credit to an outstanding countryman.

ROBIN PAGE

CHAPTER ONE

Home

When Gordon decided to work on *Beningfield's Vanishing Songbirds* it was almost like returning to his first love. Although many people associate him with butterflies, he was always interested in all aspects of English wildlife and the habitat that it needed to flourish. He was fascinated by birds and from the very early days, loved to hear the dawn chorus. As a boy, like many boys of his generation, he looked for birds' nests. He was simply enchanted by all the different aspects of birds: their flight, their beauty, their courtship and their song. I remember walking through the countryside with him on many occasions seeing and hearing the birds he loved. One of his favourites was the lapwing – the 'peewit' – and he also enjoyed seeing pheasants along the edges of the fields as we walked through the lanes. So I think that birds were his first love and then butterflies came along and flowers and everything else; he saw everything in its own context – in its habitat. He painted butterflies because they, too, were disappearing and he believed that most people did not realise how beautiful they were.

We spent many hours walking around the villages of Hertfordshire and as we walked he would hear his favourite bird – the skylark. This became one of the most important birds to him because as the song of the lark lessened and the countryside became quiet, it suggested to him that a great tragedy was taking place in our fields and meadows. As wildlife gradually disappeared and numbers plummeted so songbirds, farmland birds and garden birds were all devastated by changes in farming husbandry and pest control.

Gordon was deeply worried by what was happening – by the intensification and industrialisation of farming – because as farming 'progressed', so he saw wildlife decline and songbirds vanish. That is why this book was so important to him. He had seen birds

Tawny owl; sometimes heard from the Beningfield home.

like the barn owl, the song thrush, the skylark and the English partridge almost disappear, and tragically even as he did the first painting for this book, he was aware of the falling numbers of lapwings, swallows and skylarks – all of which he loved. To Gordon, the skylark became the symbol of the English countryside – a countryside under threat.

We moved here to Great Gaddesden in Hertfordshire twenty-seven years ago and the cottage was, and is, in a beautiful setting – although it has become noisier with the increase in traffic, and the expansion of Hemel Hempstead and the surrounding Hertfordshire towns. Our home used to be a farmworker's cottage and from it the River Gade can be seen beyond the garden, as well as a lovely area of marshy ground. The garden is very attractive too, although I think many gardeners would disagree, but it is just right for birds.

When we first came here we would often see many species from the house and even mallards and swans out there on the Gade; I still see them, kingfishers too. One of Gordon's earliest bird pictures was of a kingfisher. These paintings show that as a young artist, his work was not as defined and detailed as it became later on. He was a great admirer of both Archibald Thorburn and George Lodge, wonderful Victorian wildlife artists and their influence can be clearly seen in those early paintings.

One recent summer, I remember going to Sussex with Gordon to search for Archibald Thorburn's house. At first nobody seemed to know where the great man had lived, but eventually we found somebody who pointed out the house. The lady who lived there very kindly showed us around. Gordon was fascinated by Thorburn's studio, because it was very similar to his own. He was so pleased at the similarity that he painted a picture of Thorburn's house and studio.

An indication of the way in which bird numbers have fallen can actually be seen and heard from this house, because when we first came here there were very many house sparrows and we could always hear them chirping away. One of the names that Gordon used for them was 'spadger'. That was a common country name and spadgers could be found in every garden and every farmyard. Often they would nest under the eaves, under the tiles and they even borrowed the old nests of swallows and house martins. Strangely, the sparrow is related to the African weaver bird, but whereas the weaver bird has a beautifully woven nest, the nest of the sparrow is very untidy, consisting of straw and various materials all heaped together.

Although we have lost sparrows nesting around the cottage, we have jackdaws regularly nesting – they are trying to build in the chimney at this very moment; I can even

The house and studio of Archibald Thorburn at High Leybourne, Hascombe in Sussex.

ABOVE: *Jackdaws, the most popular members of the crow family.*
RIGHT: *The goldcrest, or 'golden crested wren', Britain's smallest bird at just 3 ½ inches long.*

hear them calling now. Gordon thought jackdaws were birds of great character, and they are probably the most popular members of the crow family because few people can claim to dislike them. They are very attractive, sociable birds with grey heads and beautiful blue eyes. They seem to have both intelligence and character and at one time they would nest in most parishes, searching out holes in trees to make their eggs and young secure. Although in some areas where the elm was once the dominant tree, jackdaw numbers seem to have fallen, in fact the population has doubled over the last twenty-five years, and they have also spread across most of mainland Britain. Some people object to them nesting in their chimneys but their call of '*jack jack*' is a real sound of traditional rural life.

It is incredible that as the jackdaw population has increased, so the numbers of house sparrows have plummeted. In the last twenty-five years the population has fallen by 64 per cent which is both worrying and amazing. I suppose it is because villages, gardens and farmyards are all so much tidier than they used to be; consequently there is not the food

for the sociable sparrow, nor are there nesting sites readily available. Sparrows were so common at the time of John Clare (1793–1864) that he wrote that the house sparrow would:

> *build a nest on the thatch under the eaves and at the gable ends of every barn and cottage. Its outside is coarsely made of hay and straw but it is painfully lined with swarms of feathers… The sparrow will breed in the hollows of willow trees and often where corn is plenty and houses are scarce on the branches of trees. Its nest then is a very large one roughly made of straws and hay as large as ones hat, lined warmly with feathers. It is in the form of a bag and the hole or entrance is on one side like the Wrens.*

Sometimes we would see Britain's smallest birds from the window. They would go into the honeysuckle and to see them we had to peep from behind the curtain. It was a challenge for Gordon to paint the goldcrest because of its fine detail. It was also once commonly known as the 'golden crested wren'. The goldcrest is just three-and-a-half inches long, the same size as the firecrest. The wren has another quarter of an inch and is three and three-quarter inches in size. All the measurements here are imperial – feet and inches, pounds and ounces, as Gordon only used the traditional measurements of this country and was totally against the imposition of the metric system.

One of his most attractive paintings is of the goldcrest, and the foliage in this one shows the way that his bird paintings developed from simple likenesses to far more detailed portraits of the bird in its habitat. It's always attractive to see goldcrests near the house and hear their distinctive, high-pitched call. WH Hudson wrote of the goldcrest that

LEFT: *The Beningfield cottage and garden with plenty of places for birds.*
RIGHT: *Blue tits – common visitors to the garden.*

Gordon's fame came from butterflies;
but he loved the whole countryside.

it had 'the smallest of small songs' – simply two notes repeated quickly two or three times and at such a high pitch that you immediately recognise it as a goldcrest, and know that it is nearby.

In winter we get more goldcrests because they migrate from mainland Europe to escape the worst of the cold. In Suffolk one of their country names is 'Tot o'er Seas' showing that this tiny little bird comes in from across the North Sea. It really is incredible that a bird just three-and-a-half inches in size can make such a journey. Often in the winter, the goldcrest is said to arrive a day or two before the woodcock and because of this another local name is 'woodcock pilot'.

The population of the goldcrest fluctuates enormously but in recent times it has seemed more secure because of all the forestry plantations and the ornamental pines and firs that have been planted; it loves conifer plantations.

The house is surrounded by ideal habitat for small birds and I still feed them regularly and can see them from the window. I enjoy watching butterflies too; they were always part of Gordon's life and with all the ivy in the garden, and near the house, brimstone butterflies do well here and were one of his favourites. I often see them flying through the garden in the summer.

We have always had pets which have been important in our lives. However, although cats are blamed for all sorts of murder and mayhem with garden birds I have to say in all honesty, that our present cat Toby is really good and prefers my company to hunting in the garden. The ginger one here was called Dad, because he was the father of Toby. They have both been very good house cats and Dad always behaved himself impeccably.

When we first moved here, we did have a cat that hunted birds but he never caught them. His name was Crispin and, incredibly, the birds that he hunted were moorhens, and he even used to jump in the River Gade to swim after them. He was a quite remarkable

cat – we have never had a swimming cat like him either before or since.

Gordon always loved deerhounds, too, and we have had three beautiful dogs: Robbie, Rory and Bruce. Gordon liked all dogs but if he had only been allowed one, he would have chosen a deerhound. He thought they made excellent companions, and although they are very big, they hardly take up any room at all when curled

LEFT: *The impeccably behaved 'Dad'.*
BELOW: *Deerhounds Robbie, Rory and Bruce.*

up small. They are well behaved and Gordon often drew them – he loved their lines, their character and their grace and beauty when they ran.

Gordon's last dog, a small terrier called Ted, made a complete contrast to the deerhounds; I still have him. He is a wonderful friend and companion but I can rarely let him loose as he would create chaos with the neighbours' cats. He gets taken for a walk most days by Barrie, and is a happy little dog, but terriers and wildlife don't go together all that well.

CHAPTER TWO

Garden

His garden, unashamedly wild and natural, was a very special place to Gordon. It was designed both to give us pleasure and give food and shelter to a wide range of wildlife. Flowers, butterflies and birds were all attracted to the garden and it was designed for all three. Gordon hated regular lawns; he thought that they should have daisies and buttercups growing in them, along with dandelions and lesser celandine. He believed that 'weeds' were part of a proper lawn and something that every country cottage ought to have — the sort of lawn where robins and blackbirds can find food and children can make daisy chains and play, and enjoy a proper country childhood.

LEFT: *Garden apples — a favourite subject and a favourite fruit for people and birds.*
RIGHT: *The robin — a rare bird that is still doing well in the garden.*

Once off the lawn Gordon did like flowers – but he liked undergrowth and nettles too and our garden was a place where harvest mice could nest and butterflies could find food for themselves as well as for their caterpillars. It was the wild plants that he loved and also the old apple trees in the orchard at the back of the cottage. He found old orchards very appealing and of course they are very good for a wide range of wildlife. The old trees attract insects and provide nesting sites, while in the spring the plum, pear and apple blossom provide nectar and pollen for bees. The fruit trees really signal the arrival of spring. As the year goes on, the seasons change and the fruit ripens – we have always allowed the wildlife to take the fruit we did not need.

We still have some old apple trees and although we used to pick large quantities of apples we also allowed some windfalls to rest on the ground so that the birds and butterflies could feed from them. Red admirals are extremely fond of fallen apples that are bruised or beginning to go rotten. Some of Gordon's loveliest paintings are of apples and butterflies; we have included one in the book; it is of a red admiral on an apple still hanging in the tree. In fact it was Gordon's love of traditional English fruit that led him to do a whole series of paintings of apples, and in the future we hope to publish them as an 'apple' book in his memory. He really believed that English apples were the best in the world. A Bramley is a wonderful cooking apple and the Cox's Orange Pippin simply cannot be beaten as an eating apple.

Of course the birds that we get in the garden after the fallen apples are redwings and fieldfares. Gordon really enjoyed painting the picture of the redwing overleaf. It actually looks cold in this picture, and I think it is one of his best. Redwings and fieldfares were very important to Gordon; he felt we should make every effort to ensure that they have enough food during the winter. This is why he was so keen for farmers and garden owners to leave their hawthorn

ABOVE: *The traditional lawn – a place for wildflowers as well as grass.*

RIGHT: *Red admiral butterfly settled on an apple.*

hedges and wild roses uncut until March, so that fieldfares and redwings, as well as thrushes and blackbirds, could eat the fruit which is so important for their survival. It really upset him to see hedges cut in late summer or early autumn so denying the birds their winter food. That is why Gordon had no problem letting surplus apples fall to the ground and it gave him great joy to see fieldfares and redwings in the garden. Another great joy was to see thrushes and blackbirds at any time. He loved them both and they certainly are among our most attractive songbirds.

As well as apples, our old orchard also has hundreds and hundreds of snowdrops in the spring which are really beautiful, and after the snowdrops come the daffodils. Gordon used to call it God's garden because it was left to nature. There are lots of forget-me-nots and celandines here at the moment and cuckoo flowers too. God's garden; it is pretty and it is a lovely garden to have and to share with wildlife.

We have always had very old Albertine roses and also the Alexandra rose which gives beautiful flowers and rose hips too. The way we managed the garden meant that there were,

LEFT: *The redwing needs garden and hedgerow fruit in winter.*
BELOW: *The wild Beningfield orchard.*

More Benigfield garden weeds.

and are, plenty of places for blackbirds and thrushes to nest and also plenty of food for them. The decline of the song thrush has been one of the great bird tragedies of our time – numbers have fallen by 66 per cent on farm land in the last twenty-five years and 52 per cent all round. This means that their numbers have fallen in gardens, woodland and on our farms. Gordon believed that the decline was caused by loss of habitat, loss of food and pesticides. Slug pellets are very bad news for song thrushes, because not only do they destroy their supply of slugs and snails, but they also poison the birds themselves. It should be remembered that the concentration of pesticides in gardens is often even greater than on farmland.

GARDEN

Chris Knights who farms in Norfolk, feels that there is another reason why thrush numbers have fallen. He believes that during dry summers there are simply fewer and fewer slugs and snails around for the thrushes to eat and feed to their young, and certainly in a dry summer you see fewer thrush anvils. In wetter summers there are more snails around and so the thrush does better. Without a doubt, the song thrush was one of Gordon's favourite birds and it also provided a link with one of his favourite writers and poets. He loved Dorset and with it the work of Thomas Hardy and he became quite an expert on his writing. Although Hardy's stories and poems were full of melancholy, *The Darkling Thrush* was a poem that greatly appealed to Gordon.

I leant upon a coppice gate
When Frost was spectre-gray,
And Winter's dregs made desolate
The weakening eye of day.
The tangled bine-stems scored the sky
Like strings of broken lyres,
And all mankind that haunted nigh
Had sought their household fires.

The land's sharp features seemed to be
The Century's corpse outleant,
His crypt the cloudy canopy,
The wind his death-lament.
The ancient pulse of germ and birth
Was shrunken hard and dry
And every spirit upon earth
Seemed fervourless as I.

At once a voice arose among
The bleak twigs overhead
In a full-hearted evensong
Of joy illimited;
An aged thrush, frail, gaunt, and small,
In blast-beruffled plume,
Had chosen thus to fling his soul
Upon the growing gloom.

So little cause for carolings
Of such ecstatic sound
Was written on terrestrial things
Afar or nigh around,
That I could think there trembled through
His happy good-night air
Some blessed Hope, whereof he knew
And I was unaware.

We still get the occasional thrush, but see a lot more blackbirds – another real songbird of British gardens. It is a pleasure to hear the dawn chorus with the blackbirds singing joyfully. Although their overall numbers have declined by 33 per cent over the last twenty-five years, we still have them in this garden in good numbers. It is surprising that thrush numbers have fallen here because we do have plenty of snails and little frogs that make ideal food for them.

Gordon was very fond of the poetry of John Clare, as well as Thomas Hardy. John Clare was known as the 'Peasant Poet' and he wrote a most attractive poem about the song of the blackbird:

…That blackbirds music from the hazel bower
Turns into golden drops this summer shower
To think the rain that wets his sutty wing
Should wake the gushes of his soul to sing
Hark at the melody how rich and loud
Like daylight breaking through the morning cloud
How luscious through that sea of green it floats

Knowest thou of music breathed from sweeter notes
Than that wild minstrel of the summer shower
Breathes at this moment from that hazel bower
To me the anthem of a thousand tongues
Were poor and idle to the simple songs
To that high toned and edifying bird
That sings to nature by itself unheard…

Long-tailed tits at their nest.

34

Birds' nests also fascinated Gordon.

Like many schoolboys, Gordon went bird nesting when he was a boy. It was always exciting looking for nests, but there was a strict rule that you could only take one egg. Lots of prominent naturalists today started their interest in this way and it was only the extravagances of the professional collectors that brought the hobby into disrepute. Although Gordon believed it was right that egg-collecting should stop, he always thought it was a shame that books on eggs and nests also disappeared through 'conservation correctness'. Knowing the type of nest and the colour of the eggs can add much interest to people watching birds in their gardens.

We get long-tailed tits in this garden and they make very attractive nests. You are extremely lucky if you can find one – they are so dainty and delicate. They are like little round balls with moss, feathers and spider's webs in them, which make them very beautiful.

John Clare describes the nest perfectly – but calls the bird 'bumbarrel' – not a very flattering name for a beautiful little bird. According to *A Dictionary of English and Folk Names of British Birds* the name bumbarrel for the 'long tailed titmouse' is from Nottinghamshire, but it obviously slipped down to John Clare's part of Northamptonshire too.

The oddling bush close sheltered – hedge new plashed
Of which springs early likeing makes a guest
First with a shade of green though winter dashed
There full as soon bumbarrels make a nest
Of mosses grey with cobwebs closely tyed
And warm and rich as feather bed within
With little hole on its contrary side

That pathway peepers may no knowledge win
Of what her little oval nest contains
Ten eggs and often twelve with dusts of red
Soft frittered – and soon the little lanes
[missing word] the young crowd and hear the twittering song
Of the old birds who call them to be fed
While down the hedge they hop and hide along

It is quite amazing that the long-tailed tits started feeding on our peanuts about six years ago and they started feeding on nuts at the Countryside Restoration Trust in Cambridgeshire at about the same time. I think it is the winter feeding of the long-tailed tits that has helped to increase their numbers. Because of the shape of the nests in Yorkshire and Norfolk the long-tailed tit is known as the Pudding Bag, while in Suffolk it used to be called Pudding Poke. It is a good description. (I used to make Gordon 'Spotted Dick' – boiled in a pudding bag – and he loved it, as he did all traditional English food.)

Sadly some birds that we once had in the garden have disappeared and we miss them. The starling is most attractive, with an amazing range of songs and sounds, but it has become very scarce and the tree sparrow has been missing for many years now.

We get many other birds in the garden though, including the great spotted woodpecker and the green woodpecker. One of the few good stories over the last twenty-five years is the way woodpecker numbers have increased. They were badly hit by the use of DDT on farmland and woodland and the very cold winter of 1962–63 really made the populations of both birds fall dramatically. With the poor breeding due to chemical poisoning and

The green woodpecker that is recovering well from chemical poisoning and loss of habitat.

the cold, and therefore lack of food, numbers plummeted; and for many years woodpeckers were absent from large areas of the country. However, over the last twenty-five years the green woodpecker has recovered and the population has grown by 92 per cent, while incredibly, the population of the great spotted woodpecker has increased by 185 per cent. It is good to hear the laughing cry of the green woodpecker again as it has been part of country life for so long. In some areas it is also known as the rain bird and when you hear that 'laughter' loud and clear it is said that rain is very near. John Clare liked the green woodpecker and there is quite an interesting piece of poetry that he wrote which both describes the woodpecker and the way that country boys at one time collected eggs.

The green woodpecker flying up and down
With wings of mellow green and speckled crown
She bores a hole in trees with crawking noise
And pelted down and often catched by boys
She makes a lither nest of grass and whool
Men fright her oft that go the sticks to pull
And stood on rotten grains to reach the hole
And as I trembled upon fear and doubt
I found the eggs and scarce could get them out
I put them in my hat a tattered crown
And scarsely without breaking brought them down
The eggs are small for such a bird they lay
Five eggs and like the sparrows spotted grey.

Another bird that comes into the garden and is very welcome is the nuthatch. Like the woodpeckers it too suffered hugely through pesticide poisoning, loss of habitat and also the cold winter of 1962–63. Again its population has increased by 82 per cent, it is good to have such an attractive bird back in the garden.

I can't remember when Gordon painted this picture of the nuthatch but it is one of his earlier works. He used to watch it closely, intrigued by the way it can travel head-first down a tree; it is the only British bird that can do this. At one time country people even believed that it perched upside down too! Another interesting characteristic of the nuthatch is that if it finds a hole in a tree trunk or wall that is too big it will make the entrance smaller with mud, until it is a better fit. This gives it the country names of

One of the most attractive garden birds, the nuthatch.

'Mud-dabber' and 'Mud-stopper'. Some years we have had a spotted flycatchers nest in the garden. Gordon was excited to see them, but they catch and eat butterflies as well as flies so he was caught in a bit of a quandary. He enjoyed seeing the birds, but he hated to see the discarded butterfly wings on the ground below the nest. So we are very lucky to have such a lovely garden and to have song birds all around us which really helped Gordon to develop his art and his appreciation for nature. I am still very lucky to live in such a beautiful place.

Of course, even in this garden there are unwelcome visitors. Gordon didn't like to see too many magpies, and he was always irritated by grey squirrels; he would chase them off, or even fire the odd shot at them because they do take both eggs and fledglings out of nests. And yes, I have to say that our cats also like the garden, but I have only seen Toby with mice. I didn't ever see Toby's father Dad, with a mouse – he was a nice cat and he really didn't get birds and he had such a bad life in the beginning. He was semi-wild and although we fed him outside for a year or so, you could never get near him. He used to sleep in the old hay wagon that we have in the garden. Then he disappeared for about six weeks and when he came back he had been caught in a snare which had cut into him, right round his middle. We managed to get him into a box and take him to the vet to be stitched up, and we brought him back and kept him in the shepherd's hut for a few weeks until he was healed and he became very tame. Once he came into the house he went out very rarely, so I don't think he affected the wildlife in our garden at all.

CHAPTER THREE

Village

Not only did Gordon enjoy living in his cottage and in the countryside but he also thought it was important to be part of the village. The whole idea of village life appealed to him because he saw villages as the focal points for people in the countryside. As you look around, it is clear that these old communities have developed over hundreds of years for specific reasons. Nearly all of them have been linked to farming and the land, and this too Gordon felt was important. He was very upset latterly at the way farming was in steep decline, because he believed that a healthy countryside and flourishing villages depended on a prosperous agriculture. He wanted responsible farming that would provide work for people and circulate money through the community. Strangely, the tragic 2001 outbreak of foot and mouth disease showed that Gordon was right. Farming is important to the whole countryside and when farming suffers, many other industries and aspects of country life also suffer. The politicians may think village life and farming are unimportant but the financial consequences of the foot and mouth outbreak showed that all country life and all country activities are interdependent.

Gordon loved the idea of village families stretching back to the time when farming was mixed and animals would wander freely down the village street. He enjoyed being part of Great Gaddesden and the way that it almost grew out of the Hertfordshire landscape fascinated him. It is a very pretty village and Gordon often walked round the parish to paint it. He served on the Parish Council for many years; he didn't necessarily like being a Parish Councillor but he felt strongly that he ought to be involved in the way the village was developing. He practised what he preached too, and whenever he went out to walk around the village he always came back with pockets full of litter because he wanted a clean and attractive countryside, and not one that was abused or simply seen as a tourist's theme park.

Great Gaddesden growing out of the Hertfordshire landscape.

He visited many different parts of the countryside and was particularly fond of Dorset and the Cotswolds. Dorset farming was based on sheep: where the village stopped, farming would start. Wherever Gordon was, he could imagine the old villagers living out their lives in the way described so well by Thomas Hardy. At Abbotsbury in Dorset, a favourite spot, the village seems to nestle into the countryside so naturally and the sheep too provide a traditional link and a traditional unity.

The villages of the Cotswolds gave him great pleasure and he enjoyed the little stone cottages that could be found in every parish. He particularly enjoyed visiting Upper and Lower Slaughter. The cottages with their little porches covered with roses and honey-suckle were all part of the traditional village scene and were ideal for birds. Birds and people have lived in harmony for generations.

You only have to look at some paintings of village scenes in summer and you can almost hear the sparrows chirping to one another and see the swallows swooping down to feed their young in their nests under the eaves of old buildings or the garden shed. Swallows are wonderful birds of the village and countryside and their recent decline of 16

RIGHT: *Abbotsbury – where the old unity of village, farm and field can still be felt.*

per cent is one that troubled Gordon deeply. Their twittering is part of the summer scene and they are amazing little birds. They are so beautiful and their whole life history is just incredible: to think that such small birds cover so many miles in migration to and from Africa. Gordon was always elated when he saw his first swallow in the spring and sorry when he saw them collecting on the telephone wires to depart. Again, John Clare summed up the swallow in his poem depicting the swallow's departure:

Emigrating swallows now
Sweep no more the green hills brow
Nor in circuits round the spring
Skim and dip their sutty wing
And no more their chimney high
Twitter round to catch the flye

ABOVE: *Lower Slaughter in the heart of the Cotswolds.*

RIGHT: *An early Beningfield portrait of a swallow.*

But with more majestic rise
Practising their exersise
And their young broods to pursue
Autumns weary journey through
Meditating travels long
Try boldest flights without a song
To leave our winters cold sojourn
And come no more till springs return.

I am really glad that we managed to find this painting of a swallow. It is an interesting and attractive painting, somewhere between the simple portrait and the more detailed paintings that came later. I am sure that if Gordon had managed to finish all the pictures he had in

mind for this book, he would have painted new pictures of swallows, swifts and house martins. They are all lovely birds and under threat as we get tidier and more suburban. Gordon was always infuriated when people knocked the nests of house martins from the walls and eaves of their houses, as he regarded house martins as beautiful additions to any house, rather than birds that might damage or dirty the paintwork. That is one of the reasons why he enjoyed his visits to the farm of Chris Knights in Norfolk, because Chris has large numbers of house martins, swallows and indeed sparrows. The reason is very simple, because he has the right habitat and conditions for them. He feeds the sparrows the whole year through, and in addition he deliberately puts down water in the spring and early summer so that the swallows and house martins have got plenty of mud to make new nests and rebuild old ones.

I suppose it is inevitable that when you think of swallows you think of cricket; and Gordon enjoyed cricket; he thought it was a wonderful game. To see the swallows

Cricket at Stanway in the Cotswolds.

hawking for flies in the outfield was always enjoyable. There is something very relaxing about cricket and like traditional country-sports it is one of those activities that bind people together from all backgrounds. That was another attraction of country life to Gordon: people from different backgrounds and classes mixing and getting on well together, and understanding the countryside, and making it work and flourish.

He was so pleased when he stumbled across this little cricket ground at Stanway in the Cotswolds. The match was in progress when he painted it, and he was amused by the fact that the outfield was ridge and furrow which made fielding very difficult. But yet the people obviously enjoyed the game and there was a lovely thatched pavilion with bikes leaning against it. Totally by coincidence, Gordon later discovered that the pavilion was donated to the village by JM Barrie, the author of *Peter Pan*.

Burnham Overy in Norfolk with its famous mill.

Although he loved Hertfordshire, Dorset and the Cotswolds, he was also attracted by East Anglia and he liked Norfolk. Again the Norfolk villages have grown from their links with the land, and he was fascinated to see the signs of that early link. He was fascinated by windmills, and Burnham Overy, the village on the north Norfolk coast with its ancient windmill, is another one of those settlements that seems to be part of the landscape. It has grown and developed with time, and in the background is the old mill and around the village are trees and meadows. It is a village surrounded by wildlife where people and birds co-exist happily. It is scene that if transformed into summer you could almost hear a whitethroat calling because of the trees and bushes and the feeling of country.

The white throat whose song is a familiar summer feature of scrub and thicket.

CHAPTER FOUR

Farm

Farms were very important to Gordon because he thought that farming gave life to villages and parishes. He believed that traditional farms were vital for a living and working countryside and if he hadn't been an artist he would probably have become a gamekeeper. Because a gamekeeper's work is dealing with birds and animals and

A traditional Kent farmyard with its oasthouses.

creating habitat for them, he regarded the life of a gamekeeper as being on a par with a wildlife warden. There's not much difference: one is looking after pheasants and partridges, but still noticing all aspects of nature and wildlife, and the wildlife warden is looking after avocets or marsh harriers or some other exotic species. They are really doing the same thing – helping to make sure that the birds in their care do well.

Although he was fascinated by farming, farms that were intensively cultivated made him very cross. He hated farms that used too many chemicals or ploughed too close to the hedgerows or ripped them out completely. He was very upset by the intensification and industrialisation of farming, as he saw it as an attack on nature. He got on very well with traditional farmers – but the big uncaring prairie farmers and intensive livestock breeders he regarded as arrogant. Gordon also enjoyed talking to farmworkers, and he believed that it was very important for farm prices to be fair so that farmworkers could stay working profitably on the land. He realised that if farmers did not make a profit, they could not afford 'conservation'.

The other thing he hated about some modern farms was their tidiness. Clean and

LEFT: *Meadow brown and ringlet thriving on 'weeds'.*

OPPOSITE: *The robin – a songbird that does well in the garden, traditional farmyard and hedgerow.*

GBeningfield

tidy farms have little wildlife, because birds need food, butterflies need weeds and all these things can be found on traditional farms. He encouraged his farming friends to leave wild corners of nettles and thistles in the farmyard, so that butterflies could breed and feed, and he urged them to retain some of the old ramshackle buildings, too, because these provide wonderful nesting sites for birds such as robins and wrens. Robins and wrens love farmyards and it is a happy coincidence that they sing well and are true songbirds of the countryside. Fortunately too, they are doing extremely well at the moment and it is encouraging to find birds that are thriving. Both the robin and wren are keen on building nests in old tractor sheds, or even old tractors. They differ slightly because the female robin builds her nest, whereas the male wren builds several nests and then leaves it up to the female to choose the one she wants. John Clare observed the robin making its nest and as usual wrote an attractive little poem about it:

A robin in full song.

> *The sparrow seeks his feathers for a nest*
> *And the fond robin with his ruddy breast*
> *Hops round the garden wall were thickly twine*
> *The leafing sweet briar and the propt woodbine*
> *And in a hole behind the thickening boughs*
> *He builds with hopeful joy his little house*
> *Stealing with jealous speed the wool and hair*
> *Were cows and sheep have lain them down to lair.*

However, the poet William Wordsworth wrote about the wren's very beautiful song and he describes it in *The Prelude*.

LEFT: *The wren – a small bird with a beautiful song.*

... that single wren
Which one day sang so sweetly in the nave
Of that old church, – though from recent showers
The earth was comfortless, and, touched by faint
Internal breezes, sobbings of the place
And respirations, from the roofless walls
The shuddering ivy dripped large drops – yet still
So sweetly 'mid the gloom the invisible bird
Sang to herself, that there I could have made
My dwelling-place, and lived for ever there
To hear such music.

Other birds too like old farms buildings and blackbirds will build in sheds and old bits of machinery. Gordon was greatly amused when a blackbird actually built its nest in the car engine belonging to the tenant farmer of the Countryside Restoration Trust, Tim Scott. It meant that Tim could not drive his car until the female had hatched her eggs and the young birds had fledged.

FARM

I am sure that one of the birds that Gordon would have loved to have painted was the chaffinch. Chaffinch numbers are increasing, and the bird gets its name because at one time it loved to hop around in the chaff found in farmyards. Sadly many people have forgotten what chaff is – it is the outside husk of the grain. Gordon remembered the old scenes of men threshing and it was the young boy on threshing day who was always put in charge of the chaff where it came out of the drum. It was the dustiest, and dirtiest job of all and so the experienced men always gave the youngsters that task. In southern Britain it is worth saying too that chaff is pronounced 'charf', and so the southern pronunciation of chaffinch is 'charffinch'.

As well as buildings, and chaff, animals are a real part of traditional farming. Even here around Hemel Hempstead we are lucky to have a herd of Belted Galloways on Boxmoor Trust land which are a very attractive and hardy breed of cattle. A mixed farm has hens, sheep and cows, and normally a cockerel or two crowing. That too Gordon found amazing and irritating, that as the make up of villages changed so incomers complained of cocks crowing in the local farmyard, and even cows mooing! He found this very sad, and serious. He believed that, like intensive farming, the objection to cocks crowing showed that people were getting further and further away from nature, their roots and traditional country life.

When he went to Dorset, Gordon searched for sheep and the old sheep walks and grasslands of Dorset. One of his favourite breeds of sheep was the Dorset Horn – such a beautiful animal, it has been a feature of Dorset life for many generations. At the time of Hardy, the Dorset Horn would have been very common throughout Dorset.

In Hertfordshire at one time we had many shepherds and sheep and in Gordon's early years he painted them. We have an old shepherd's hut in the garden. He also started to collect the old tools of shepherding such as shepherds' crooks, lanterns and sheep bells.

RIGHT: *The cockerel – the sound of a rural morning.*
BELOW: *Dorset Horn sheep.*

Around many traditional farmyards there are also old orchards and so bullfinches can usually be seen. The pair of bullfinches here make up one of the pictures that Gordon painted specifically for this book, and it really is one of his best. The bullfinch is a very beautiful bird, but it is in steep decline; the population has fallen by 62 per cent. Undoubtedly the disappearance of orchards and weeds from farmyards has accounted for this fall in numbers. The bullfinch has a bad reputation for eating the

BELOW: *A traditional sheepherding scene, now almost gone.*

RIGHT: *A pair of bullfinches – one of Gordon's last paintings.*

buds off fruit trees, but it also eats many other seeds, such as the seeds of nettle and dock, bramble and ash, and so a traditional farmyard will be the natural place for it. John Clare wrote:

> *... the bullfinch is a beautiful bird the plumage is fine and its shape tho rather heavy is commanding and noble it begins to build in may its nest is an odd curious one nearly flat made in a negligent manner of small sticks and lined with morsels of fine twitch and roots it generally builds in a thick clump of Briars or blackthorn*

…its song is rather varied and pretty it is a great destroyer of the buds of fruit trees in winter like the black and blue Tit-mouse and its fine plumage and pretty song cannot make any petition for its crime to the enraged gardiner who shoots it with the others indiscriminately – in winter it frequents gardens and orchards and in spring it returns to its wild solitudes of woods and commons were it can feed in saftey …

The barn owl – now breeding again at the CRT's Lark Rise Farm.

The other famous bird of the farmyard is the barn owl, or white owl, and Gordon would have been overjoyed to know that barn owls have returned to Lark Rise Farm, thanks to the work of the Countryside Restoration Trust. When the Trust acquired its first piece of land in 1993 it was prairie, as were the later acquisitions, and Gordon was really happy about the way the CRT was encouraging wildlife to return. The reappearance of the barn owl would also have confirmed his theory that farming and wildlife can flourish hand in hand if given the opportunity.

Over the years, the barn owl has had a very rough time. It suffered enormously because of pesticide use which damaged its breeding capability. In addition to this much of the habitat for small mammals – its staple diet – also disappeared and so food became scarce and then the mania for smartening up old buildings also meant that its traditional barn nesting sites became scarce. Gordon believed that far too many old buildings were being done up as executive housing. Another casualty of the 'barn conversion' is the ordinary house sparrow.

Of course barn owls can also nest in holes in trees, but when the elm disappeared it meant that natural nesting sites were vanishing too. Fortunately the slide has been

ABOVE: *Blue tit and sparrows. Both thrive on traditional farms.*
RIGHT: *Farm birds need weeds. Hogweed provides flowers, attracting insects and birds.*

stabilised and, as can be seen at Lark Rise Farm, if given the opportunity the barn owl can make a comeback. It is a very beautiful bird, and one day I looked out of my window here, and there was even one on my washing line. I don't know how it got there or what it was doing. It didn't stay long but I really enjoyed seeing it.

Gordon would have been very worried about what is happening to small farms today and we can only hope that the 2001 foot and mouth epidemic will mean that politicians give more sympathy and understanding to farming. They must ensure that the traditional family farm, with its wildlife and its care for the land, has a future.

CHAPTER FIVE

Field

It was seeing the way in which our countryside, fields and hedgerows had become so empty that made Gordon desperately keen to produce this book. His anxiety grew steadily as the birds and the wildlife he loved gradually vanished, or became scarce, in the fields and along the hedgerows where he had first become interested in nature. It depressed and worried him so much that he wanted to do this book both as a tribute to our wonderful songbirds and as a desperate plea to those people who control farming and the countryside – the politicians – to change direction. He considered that the activities of man were, and are, responsible for the destruction of wildlife and that the actions of people, politicians, farmers and everybody interested in the countryside could put things right again. That is why he was so pleased to become a founder Trustee of the Countryside Restoration Trust, and President of Butterfly Conservation. He regarded countryside restoration as the future, and that restoration was the conservation of the future. He often went to wildlife reserves but he thought that for nature to have a chance it had to get back to the general countryside where it had been when he was a boy, and when he was a young man, developing his skills as an artist.

It makes frightening reading to see the list of birds that have declined over the last twenty-five years, many of which appear in this book, and almost certainly if Gordon had still been here, he would have included pictures of all the birds on this list because he worried so much about them. The turtle dove, the grey wagtail, the yellow wagtail, the tree sparrow, the willow warbler. He would have wanted to have drawn and painted them to try and make more people appreciate their beauty, and the beauty of their songs, in an effort to get things changed for the better.

The skylark – symbol of a healthy countryside and logo of the Countryside Restoration Trust.

65

Redpoll – down 92%
Tree sparrow – down 87%
Corn bunting – down 85%
English partridge (grey) – down 82%
Turtle dove – down 77%
Marsh tit – down 69%
Spotted flycatcher – down 68%
Willow tit – down 63%
Starling – down 58%
Lapwing – down 52%
Skylark – down 52%
Reed bunting – down 52%
Yellowhammer – down 43%
Grey wagtail – down 39%
Linnet (in-it) – down 38%
Willow warbler – down 23%
Dunnock (hedge sparrow) –
    down 21%
Mistle thrush – down 21%
Meadow pippit – down 20%
Swallow – down 16%
Yellow wagtail – down 13%
Cuckoo – down 12%
French (red-legged) partridge – down 6%
Greenfinch – down 2%

Figures from the British Trust for Ornithology

From the figures here, the 'Lark Ascending' has become the 'Lark Descending'.

I suppose the bird whose decline symbolised to Gordon the destruction caused by the industrialisation of farming more than any other was the skylark. I remember wandering through the fields with him as the lark sang and often he would look for the nests as we walked. They are very difficult to find, but he would find them occasionally. There would be hares too, he loved to see them both, and of course just as skylark numbers have plummeted so have hare numbers. It thrilled him to walk over Lark Rise Farm after just a matter of two or three years, and hear skylarks again as he had done when he was a young man, and to see the brown hare in its March madness, and the leverets running through the stubble. Their return was so swift that it gave him hope for the future.

He painted the skylark picture at the start of this chapter especially for the book and so it is very special; it is in such detail. He was so pleased to go and see a nest in Leicestershire on the Game Conservancy's farm and I think it captures the spirit of the countryside and farmland.

He loved the poetry and music linked to the skylark too, and the *Lark Ascending* by Vaughan Williams was one of his favourite pieces of music; he felt it was so descriptive of the lark's flight and song. When in his last few weeks in hospital one of the nurses kindly gave him a small tape recorder with headphones, and the tape of *Lark Ascending*, he spent many hours listening to this, eyes closed, with a peaceful look on his face – completely transported. We had it played at his Memorial Service in St Albans Abbey. On that great organ it sounded wonderful. Listening to it takes you mentally into the middle of a field on a hot sunny day, and you can hear the lark singing as it goes higher and higher. John Clare catches the same feeling with his words:

> *… And still I love the ground lark's flight*
> *Starting up the ploughman's height*
> *And more and more unseal his eye*
> *To see the skylark as he springs*
> *Shake morning's moisture from his wings*
> *And rise and sing in music proud*
> *Small as bee beneath a cloud…*

There is so much beautiful poetry about larks and Gordon had many favourite pieces. He loved Shelley's *To a Skylark*, which is too long to reprint in its entirety. It starts:

> *Hail to thee, blythe spirit!*
> *Bird thou never wert,*
> *That from heaven, or near it,*
> *Pourest thy full heart*
> *In profuse strains of unpremeditated art.*
>
> *Higher still and higher*
> *From the earth thou springest*
> *Like a cloud of fire;*
> *The blue deep thou wingest,*
> *And singing still dost soar and soaring ever singest…*

George Meredith's *The Lark Ascending* was another favourite.

He rises and begins to round,
He drops the silver chain of sound,
Of many links without a break,
In chirrup, whistle, slur and shake,
All intervolved and spreading wide,
Like water-dimples down a tide
Where tipple ripple overcurls
And eddy into eddy whirls;
A press of hurried notes that run
So fleet they scarce are more than one,
Yet changeingly the trills repeat
And linger ringing while they fleet,
Sweet to the quick o' the ear, and dear
To her beyond the hand maid ear,
Who sits beside our inner springs,
Too often dry for this he brings,
Which seems the very jet of earth
At sight of sun, her music's mirth,
As up he winds the spiral stair,
A song of light, and pierces air
With fountain ardour, fountain play,
To reach the shining tops of day,
And drink in everything discerned
An ecstasy to music turned,
Impelled by what his happy bill
Disperses; drinking, showering still,
Unthinking save that he may give
His voice the outlet, there to live
Renewed in endless notes of glee,
So thirsty of his voice is he,
For all to hear and all to know
That he is joy, awake, aglow,
The tumult of the heart to hear
Through pureness filtered crystal-clear,

And know the pleasure sprinkled bright
By simple singing of delight,
Shrill, irreflective, unrestrained,
Rapt, ringing, on the jet sustained,
Without a break, without a fall,
Sweet silvery, sheer lyrical,
Perennial, quavering up the chord
Like myriad dews of sunny sward
That trembling into fulness shine,
And sparkle dropping argentine.

John Clare also describes the skylark in prose.

> *The sky lark is a slender light bird with a coppld crown on the head builds its nest on the ground and lays five or six spotted eggs this is the one celebrated by poets for the sweetness of its song they gather in flocks after harvest and are caught in some parts by nets thrown at night in great quantitys*
>
> *The ground lark (corn bunting) is a much larger bird more solitary and less common than the other it has no song it sits on the top twigs of odd trees and bushes in spring quivering its wings and uttering a pleasant 'cree creeing' note…*

In his earlier poem John Clare's mention of the ploughman reminds me of the old saying: 'Merry larks are ploughman's clocks'. This is because when you get up very early in the morning (and when Gordon was on painting trips he often had to leave at dawn, just before first light in summer) the larks would be singing. That would be when the farmworkers were getting up for work in the old days. Another saying says 'Rise with the lark and go to bed with the lamb', meaning that you should get up early and go to bed early.

Another bird that Gordon often hoped to see, which once bred in almost every farming parish, was the lapwing – it is also known as the green plover and the peewit. Peewit comes from its very distinctive and attractive call. In the spring when the males are doing their beautiful display flight then the peewit changes to a wonderful piping call which at one time would be heard every spring. The lapwing is a beautiful bird and the colours are really quite stunning. Gordon loved lapwings at any time and to see them

LEFT: *The lapwing – another 'indicator' bird in steady decline.*

breeding during the summer and the flocks coming in during the winter always pleased him enormously.

The decline of the lapwing is a tragedy. They lay their eggs on the ground and with the mechanisation of farming they don't stand a chance. Winter wheat has also meant that conditions are no longer suitable for nesting and this is sad. Before farming became such a rapid process, if the ploughman found a nest as he was ploughing he would stop and move the eggs onto a freshly ploughed furrow, and within a few minutes the bird would be back sitting on her old eggs in the new nest which would just be a hollow in the ground.

It is incredible, too, that there are still people to be found who used to eat lapwing's eggs in spring because the bird was so common. An idea of their status is give by John Clare:

… they are as common as crows here in spring they lay on the ground and make no nest but use a horse footing or any hollow they can find they lay four eggs of an olive green color splashed with large black spots and the narrow points of the eggs are always laid inwards they have a way of decoying any thing from their young or nest by swooping and almost tumbling over them as if wounded and going to fall uttering their harsh screaming note but when near the nest they are silent and flye off in another direction which is always a signal to the old egg hunters that the nest is at hand shepherds with us train their dogs to find them often getting as much as 3d apiece for the eggs the young run as soon as they are out of the shells – Peewits are easily tamed and are often kept in gardens where they are said to do much good by destroying the slugs and worms on which they feed …

LEFT AND ABOVE: *The goldfinch is one of Britain's most beautiful and melodic birds and Gordon enjoyed painting them.*

All is not gloom and doom however, Gordon thought that goldfinches were wonderful birds, they were a favourite, and the goldfinch is one of the few song-birds and farmland birds that has actually increased in number over the last twenty-five years. It has increased by 10 per cent, although it is difficult to understand quite why as there are far fewer thistles around than there used to be – yet obviously the goldfinch is able to find enough food. Gordon was asked to paint the goldfinch many times because it is such a beautiful bird and it also has an attractive song – reasons which led to its being trapped and put in cages in the past. Along with the linnet, it was a favourite cage-bird of gypsies as John Clare noted:

The goldfinch is well known its song and beautiful plumage like the fair face of woman proves its enemy and is the cause of making it a prisoner for life it is among the most frequent and commonest of cage birds it builds its nest on the eldern or apple tree and makes its outside of grey moss like the pinks which it greatly resembles but its lining is different and instead of cowhair it prefers thistle down it lays 5 pale eggs thinly sprinkled with feint red spots in spring it pleasures the cottager with its song beside his door in the eldern tree and apple by the orchard pails it feed in summer on the groundsel seed and the broad leafd plantain when it has raisd its family they all live happily together parents and childern till the next spring and may be seen in such companys in winter tracing the common and the fallow fields were the thistles are in plenty on the seed of which it feeds till summer returns with its other food – it is not uncommon while walking down a green lane in early spring to see it perched on the top of a thistle picking out the seed or pulling the soft down for its nest and flying into the neighbouring hedge at the approach of a passer-bye.

Goldfinches were protected many years ago and it is good to know that they are still increasing. Gordon would often say that many people didn't realise how beautiful the goldfinch was until he had painted the picture in detail – they simply didn't look closely enough – the painting made them realise just what a wonderful bird it was. When they saw it they would say: 'Ooh it's lovely!' and Gordon would say, 'Well it's there all the time in your garden. Why don't you see its beauty out there where you can see it every day?'

One thing Gordon liked about the goldfinch was that it depends on weeds for its food and it loves thistledown and dandelion clocks. Consequently the habitat for the goldfinch is also good for many other species. Gordon often painted thistledown and dandelions and it really emphasises that many different types of Britain's wildlife need wild places to live and thrive. Consequently the areas that are good for goldfinches are also good for butterflies and for small mammals.

The orange tip butterfly thrives where there are flowers and weedy corners in the field, and the picture here of the orange tip on red campion again shows Gordon painting one of his favourite butterflies, and it demonstrates clearly the delicacy of his work.

The orange tip, one of Gordon's favourite butterflies.

One of my favourite paintings is of the brimstone on the thistledown; again it demonstrates that goldfinches and butterflies often go for the same wild areas along the edges of the fields. It doesn't end with butterflies either, because again one of our most attractive mice depends on the rough edges of the fields and meadows to build its nest and survive. This is the harvest mouse and Gordon searched them out to paint them. Like many farmland birds, the harvest mouse has become extremely scarce. It is a beautiful little animal with small ears and gingery fur and it also has a long prehensile tail that helps steady it as it climbs through the long stalks. Gordon was so pleased when after just two or three years the Countryside Restoration Trust had harvest mice back in its restored meadows, and it was fascinating to find that where a spinney was planted, harvest mice were nesting in the tree guards. When the volunteers checked the guards they found the beautiful little woven nests inside, presumably because the guards were both

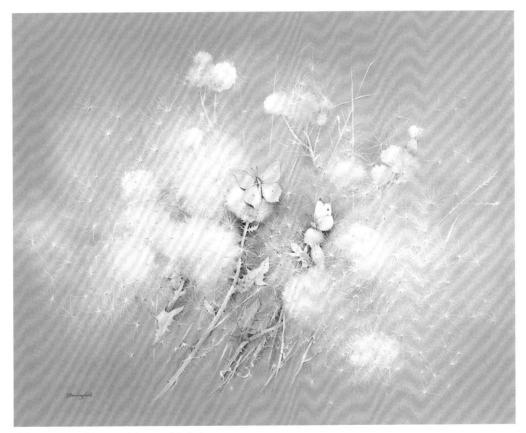

Brimstone and large white on thistledown.

warm and gave protection against the rain and wind.

Harvest mice are important too for barn owls, and so it is a cycle where everything that is part of nature depends on something else. The goldfinches depend on the thistle, the butterflies depend on the thistle flowers, the flycatchers depend on the butterflies, the mice depend on the long grasses and flowers, and the barn owls depend on the mice. Everything is interdependent, and if one part of the circle is broken then the circle is broken for all the species concerned. Gordon really felt this deeply and so he wanted good healthy farming so that everything could survive and flourish as it had once.

He did paint a bird that he had never seen. It was the corncrake; a bird that was once common in most of the parishes in Britain. It is again interesting to note that one of the fields next to Lark Rise Farm had corncrakes in them between the First and Second World Wars, as old villagers there can remember hearing them. But now the nearest corncrakes to those fields are hundreds of miles away in the Inner Hebrides although it is said that occasional birds are heard and seen in the north of England and in Scotland. Incredibly for two summers running corncrakes have again been heard on Lark Rise Farm.

LEFT AND RIGHT: *Harvest mice can still do well in arable edges if grass and 'weeds' are allowed to grow.*

FIELD

LEFT: *The corncrake – almost gone – but on the point of recovery?*

It is assumed that they were birds migrating away from Britain for the winter, but we hope that one day a pair will decide to stay as the restored hay meadows are perfect for them.

Though numbers have been small for sometime, the RSBP is helping with schemes in the Hebrides to delay the cutting of hay so that the birds can breed and the populations can be saved. The corncrake has a very distinctive call; like somebody running their thumbnail along a comb twice in quick succession. It is a remarkable bird that flies rather like a moorhen and crouches and creeps around in the long grasses and crops; sadly when the harvesters and cutters come along, the bird can be killed. It is a problem that has been building up for many years, and once more John Clare even suggests that a problem existed when the farmworkers cut their fields with scythes.

We hear it in the weeding time
When knee deep waves the corn
We hear it in the summers prime
Through meadows night and morn

And now I hear it in the grass
That grows as sweet again
And let a minutes notice pass
And now tis in the grain.

Yet accident will often meet
The nest within its way
And weeders when they weed the wheat
Discover where they lay

And mowers on the meadow lea
Chance on their noisey guest
And wonder what the bird can be
That lays without a nest

In simple holes that birds will rake
When dusting on the ground
They drop their eggs of curious make
Deep blotched and nearly round

A mystery still to men and boys
Who know not where they lay
And guess it but a summer noise
Among the meadow hay

Sadly the old scarecrow is almost redundant in some areas.

But of course there other fields besides grass fields and corn fields and it is again an indication of what has happened to our wildlife that the water meadows and rough meadows are still disappearing. Gordon liked visiting the old water meadows so suitable for corncrakes and yellow wagtails in Hardy country, and he liked the wonderful meadows and hedges close to Lark Rise Farm too.

Now, with the decline of farmland birds, it seems incredible that once there were scarecrows in every field to frighten off the birds. There are

LEFT: *English (grey) partridges, the sign of a healthy farm.*

80

Pheasants are always welcome in woodland or at the field edge.

still crows and pigeons to be kept off some crops but the beautiful old fashioned scare-crows have become almost as scarce as the skylark. On one occasion, however, Gordon did find a wonderful old scarecrow and he couldn't resist drawing it.

Another part of the wildlife circle is also missing in arable crops. They were once full of wild flowers which produced insects ideal for young skylarks and also young pheasants and partridges. So there has been a bird decline in our meadows and in our arable fields as well. Gordon loved to see partridges and pheasants and it always gave him great pleasure to see partridges at the edge of fields; the English partridge is a very beautiful bird. He enjoyed pheasants too; both on the plate and in the field, and a good wild partridge and pheasant population is an indicator of good farming practices.

One of the methods of getting skylarks and English partridges back practiced on Lark Rise Farm is to have unsprayed field edges around some of the arable crops – 'unsprayed headlands' – this means that poppies and other wild flowers known by the pesticide manufacturers as 'weeds', can provide both colour and habitat for insects and this in turn means survival for the chicks and an attractive landscape. Again, at Lark Rise Farm, as harvest approaches, some of the headlands look absolutely spectacular with poppies and all sorts of other broadleaved flowers and weeds. Certainly this is one of the reasons birds, butterflies and insects are coming back in most encouraging numbers. It is a technique pioneered by the Game Conservancy, and if only these innovations could be introduced to all our farmland our wildlife would come back very quickly and larks would again be singing over almost every field.

LEFT: *The wildflower harvest of an 'unsprayed headland'.*

CHAPTER SIX

Hedgerow

Gordon regarded hedgerows as one of the most vital features of the British countryside – important both from a landscape perspective and for the preservation of wildlife. They give protection, provide nesting sites and, of course, produce food for a wide range of birds, animals and insects. In addition to this, he realised that they had an agricultural function and he saw a properly managed hedge as far more efficient and attractive than a fence.

For all these reasons, Gordon became very depressed in the 1960s, and 1970s when it became a farming fashion – encouraged by subsidies – to rip out hedges quite needlessly. He believed that the removal of hedges showed just how environmentally illiterate politicians and the bureaucrats from the Ministry of Agriculture, Fisheries and Food had become. To him, the vanishing hedge was a sign that people were becoming cut off from nature – every bulldozer he saw, every chainsaw he heard, caused him much sadness. He condemned, too, the big farmers who went along with farming fashion and the small farmers who followed them, just for the subsidy.

The disappearance of the hedge is not something that can be blamed on all farmers but on the farming establishment and the followers of fashion. Even since those days of hedgerow vandalism, the destruction of hedges has continued, gradually spreading throughout the countryside. Several times it upset Gordon so much that he actually confronted the farmer doing it. I suppose the polite way to describe what ensued was that they had a 'difference of opinion' or a 'colourful discussion'.

Of course some people will say that thousands of miles of new hedges have been planted over the past few years. That is true, but a new hedge does not have the wildlife

The hedgerow and hedgerow tree – important ingredients in the 'traditional English landscape'.

habitat of an old hedge. An old mature hedge has everything that wildlife needs: it protects from wind and rain, it gives security for the young, and as a source of food, the hedgerow is the most productive there can be. Hedges too can cover a wide variety of shapes and sizes from a small trimmed hedge, to a laid hedge that keeps cattle and sheep inside the field, and great sprawling, straggling hedges that have long since lost their agricultural use but are there as landscape features. Some hedges in the past were just parish boundaries and they too were immensely rich in mature trees and bushes. Alongside the hedges there are flowers and clumps of rough grasses and in the spring there are swathes of Queen Anne's Lace (cow parsley) and a whole host of wild flowers and wild plants from red campion, cuckoo flower, hedge garlic and of course several types of violets.

The other activity that Gordon hated was when farmers started cutting their hedges in the summer and at harvest time, in so doing they removed all the hedgerow harvest that should have been feeding the birds during the winter. It is another farming fashion; obviously some farmers prefer tidiness to seeing fieldfares, redwings, mistle thrushes, blackbirds and song thrushes in the hedgerows during the winter. Hedgerows make great highways for wildlife and in these days of roads, development and intensive agriculture hedgerows provide the link so that wildlife can spread throughout the countryside. If grassland and hedgerows are ploughed up then the wildlife and the habitat it needs becomes trapped – it can become like an island. Hedgerows can link spinney to wetland and hedgerow to heath allowing nature to spread across the land.

One of the many reasons that Gordon often visited Bird's Farm, which now has Lark Rise Farm next to it, was because of some of the great straggling hedges and the huge variety of berries and fruits that could be found. He really considered the berries and the crab apples to make up a wild harvest and he loved to paint them.

This painting of hedgerow fruit is from one of the best hedges at Bird's Farm and in just a very small stretch it is possible to find hops, hips, haws, blackberries, dogwood, buckthorn, crab apples and briony. Consequently such hedgerows are very important for keeping birds alive during the winter months. But it is not just birds that are attracted to the hedgerow harvest because animals also appear. Woodmice are really attractive little creatures and once the blackberries are ripe they too clamber up into the hedge to eat the fruit. They are bigger than house mice, and their coats seem shinier and their eyes brighter. On a blackberry picking expedition it is often possible to find a little mouse sticking its head out of the foliage as if to say: 'What are you doing, stealing my blackberries?'

Part of the hedgerow harvest at Bird's Farm.

Wood mice (left) and comma (right) both enjoying ripe blackberries.

Gordon was very interested when Robin Page saw a hobby fly past his study window with a mouse in its talons. Hobbys are amazing little birds of prey, and normally they take small birds and dragonflies. They have even been known to take swallows and swifts on the wing, but Robin actually saw one fly by clutching a mouse. Initially we thought he was hallucinating or he had been at the cowslip wine again, but on talking to experts it seems that there have been several confirmed incidents of hobbys taking small mammals.

Even butterflies like blackberries; a nice juicy blackberry will attract the red admiral, the peacock, the tortoiseshell, the comma. The flowers and fruit of the blackberry are also favourites of the gatekeeper.

The habitat around the hedgerows is also very good for butterflies and I have included here the brimstone. It was always, without exception, the first butterfly to fly in the spring. On a warm March day or early April, Gordon would say; 'It seems like a brimstone day today' and then the brimstone would appear in the garden or along the hedgerow.

I must again mention the bullfinch, because bullfinches love the fruit and even the seeds of blackberries, and when the fruit dries up the bullfinch will still go onto the hedge and eat the seeds. A picture like the one overleaf, with a beautiful hedge, the bullfinch and the blackberries would probably take Gordon a fortnight, or even longer, to paint, because it is in such great detail. I think this picture, a combination of bird and fruit, shows his great affection for the countryside and the way in which he wanted to show the beauty of the things that we are in danger of losing for ever.

One of the birds that loves hedgerows is the linnet. It was always fun going into the countryside with Gordon because he had a wonderful sense of humour and every year I would hear: 'O look, there's a bush with a linnet in-it'. The painting of a pair of linnets, over the page, again shows his love for both the bird and the hedgerow. The linnet is a beautiful bird and its numbers are decreasing rapidly. It likes eating seeds and it is a bird of field and hedgerow. It is a sociable bird too. Linnets will nest quite close together in places where numbers are still healthy and will travel around in little parties in the winter and they enjoy roosting together. Like the goldfinch, the linnet was a very popular caged bird which explains why its numbers fell so drastically in the nineteenth century. When bird trapping was at its height, a caged linnet could be found in numerous gypsy caravans and country cottages because of its beauty and the beauty of its song. Fortunately, those days are past and we hope too that the days will pass when unthinking farmers and politicians oversee the destruction of the linnet's habitat.

In many parts of the country, the linnet was known as the gorse-bird, whin-linnet, furze-bird or gorse-linnet, because whin and furze are other names for gorse. The linnet is particularly attracted to wasteland with gorse, and thistles and so it became associated with the gorse. The other picture overleaf is of the linnet on gorse – it is the furze bird.

John Clare once more hit the nail on the head about the linnet and it is astonishing how accurate his observations were of wildlife:

… brown linnet or furze linnet builds in furze bushes on heaths makes a nest of dead grass lined with rabbit fur lays 5 eggs somthing like the former but smaller sprinkled with red and purple spots at the large end – great destroyers of turnip seed of which they are very fond and it will attract them for miles their song is beautiful they are often called furze larks by the bird catchers and are eroniosly considered as different birds the cock bird has a beautiful flush of red on its breast.

Another bird of hedgerow, driftway and old drove road is the yellowhammer. As I walked through the countryside with Gordon we loved to hear its song of 'a little bit of bread and no cheese'. It was, and should be, a part of the countryside and it is one of our most beautiful birds. It always surprised Gordon that some people would go rushing off to Africa and exotic places to see beautiful birds, but if they only stopped to look at some of our own birds they would be surprised

ABOVE: *A hedge with a linnet in-it.*

at just how beautiful and vivid they are too. A male yellowhammer in full breeding plumage must be one of the most beautiful birds anywhere. They have been terribly hit by 'efficient' farming and it was one of Gordon's great joys to see them coming back in good numbers at Lark Rise Farm. Not only did he see linnets and yellowhammers at Lark Rise Farm but corn buntings and reed buntings too. Of course the yellowhammer is a bunting and sometimes it is called 'yellow bunting'. One of its country names is 'scribbling lark' because of the pattern on the egg. (It looks as if somebody with a fine, but runny pen has scribbled all over the eggshell – hence its name.) Gordon would have been pleased by the fact that last summer on the Countryside Restoration Trust's set-aside,

LEFT: *The linnet loves gorse – giving it the country name of gorse-linnet and furze-linnet.*

Robin found a yellowhammer's nest on the ground within about half a minute of walking onto it. The nest can be found on the ground or very low down. I had better say that Robin then left the set-aside quickly so as not to disturb the other yellowhammers, skylarks and grey partridges that were often seen on that field during the summer breeding season. John Clare's description of the yellowhammer again makes interesting reading:

> *... a bold bird builds its nest on the ground and in low bushes of dead grass and twitch and lines it with horse hair lays five eggs of a fleshy ash color streaked all over with black crooked lines as if done with a pen and for this it is often called the 'writing lark' and thought by birdnesting boys to be a different bird from the yellow hamer it likes to build in banks facing the sun by dykes etc...*

In John Clare's writing 'twitch' is the common country name for that terrible weed of field and garden – couch grass.

ABOVE AND RIGHT: *An early yellowhammer (above) and a more recent yellowhammer (right), showing how Gordon's technique developed.*

94

Whereas the yellowhammer and the linnet have a most attractive song, the corn bunting hasn't much of song at all. But nevertheless it is an attractive bird. Out of interest I have included John Clare's description of a corn bunting.

Close where the milking maidens pass
In roots and twitches drest
Within a little bunch of grass
A groundlark made her nest
The maiden touched her with her gown
And often frit her out
And looked and set her buckets down
But never found it out
The eggs where large and spotted round
And dark as is the fallow ground
The schoolboy kicked the grass in play
But danger never guest
And when he came to mow the hay
They found an empty nest

The reed bunting is another very attractive bird which has returned to Lark Rise Farm; although I have included it in the hedgerow chapter, it can be found in marshy places and reed beds and it was once called the 'reed sparrow'. On Lark Rise Farm the reed buntings have come back along an old ditch with scrub growing on the banks. Again, although the book is called *Vanishing Songbirds* the reed bunting's song appears to have vanished, or at least it is not very good. Its jumble of notes sounds almost as if it has forgotten the tune, but it is an important and very attractive bird, particularly the male, and so I thought it was right to include it here. At a reduction of 52 per cent it is a rapidly disappearing bird, but where there are conservationists working hard in conjunction with farmers the trend has been reversed. John Clare noted that the 'reed sparrow':

is a brown slender bird with a black head and has some resemblance to the sparrow
it haunts lakes and marshy places and builds a curious nest among the dead reed or on
the bank by the side of the water always choosing a place that is difficult to come at its
nest is made of dead grass and always lined with the down of the reed it lays 5 eggs and

LEFT: *The reed bunting, still doing well where farmers leave scrubby ditch-sides and boggy field edges.*

sometime six eggs not much unlike the white throats but larger of a dirty white freckled with brown and purple spots at the large end they are solitary birds and are seldom seen more than two together they have sort of Song but not fine or varied

The cuckoo is another bird that is difficult to place – woodland or hedgerow? The truth is that the cuckoo is a bird of all sorts of places as it searches for a nest in which to lay its eggs. It will go over reed beds looking for the nests of sedge and reed warblers, it will go into gardens looking for the nests of hedge sparrows and blackbirds; it will go along hedgerows too, searching for any nests that are available and, of course, it will turn up in woods as well. Gordon would get very excited when he heard the first cuckoo of the year and he would ring up his friends in the hope that he was first to hear it. It is a real sound of summer although it seems to be becoming more and more scarce. If the decline keeps on, it will be a tragedy as the cuckoo is part of the tradition, folklore and sound of an English summer. Everybody knows the little line:

> *The cuckoo comes in April*
> *He sings his song in May,*
> *In the middle of June he changes tune*
> *And in July – he flies away.*

There is another interesting little verse from Norfolk:

> *If the cuckoo lights on a bare bough,*
> *Keep your hay and sell your cow.*
> *But if he comes on the blooming may,*
> *Keep your cow and sell your hay.*

It is fascinating to note the reaction of songbirds when the cuckoo appears. Many seem to mistake it for a sparrowhawk, and they are wise to do so, because although the cuckoo is not looking for them, it is looking for their nests:

ABOVE AND RIGHT: *The cuckoo; the sound of summer, but the sound is getting fainter.*

BENINGFIELD'S VANISHING SONGBIRDS

The cuckoo like a hawk in flight
With narrow pointed wings
Wews oer our heads – soon out of sight
And as she flies she sings
And darting down the hedge row side
She scar[e]s the little bird
Who leaves the nest it cannot hide
While plaintive notes are heard

I've watched it on an old oak tree
Sing half an hour away
Untill its quick eye noticed me
And then it whewed away
Its mouth when open shone as red
As hips upon the briar
Like stock doves seemed its wings and head
But striving to get nigher

It heard me and above the trees
Soon did its flight pursue
Still waking summers melodies
And singing as it flew
So quick it flies from wood to wood
Tis miles off ere you think it gone
I've thought when I have listening stood
Full twenty sang – when only one

When summer from the forrest starts
Its melody with silence lies
And like a bird from foreign parts
It cannot sing for all it tries
'Cuck, cuck' it cries and mocking boys
Crie 'Cuck' and then it stutters more
Till quite forgot its own sweet voice
It seems to know itself no more

John Clare

The beautiful song of the mistle thrush
is one of the early signs of spring.

100

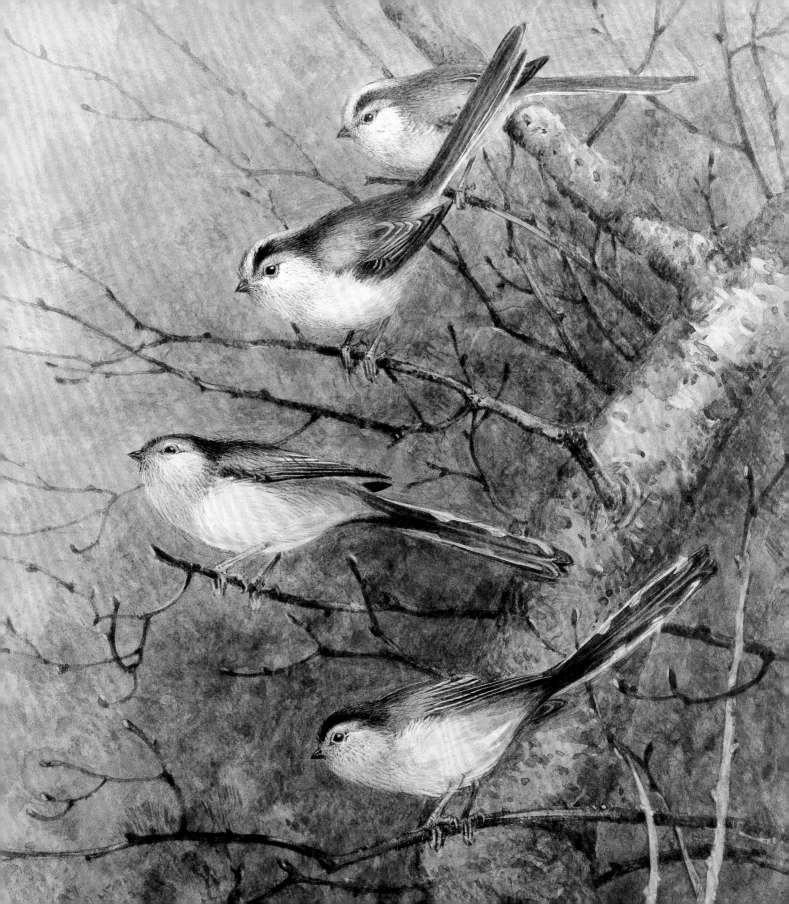

In total contrast to the cuckoo on leafy branches in full summer, is one of Gordon's favourite birds: the mistle thrush. It sings from the tallest tree in the hedgerow, an oak or an ash; it is one of the earliest birds to sing, as spring approaches, and so the mistle thrush will be singing on bare branches before many other birds have started. It seems to be saying, 'This is my tree, this is my area, I have my wife about here somewhere and she is going to nest and lay her eggs.' The mistle thrush is bigger than the song thrush and flies faster and it seems to be more aggressive. Consequently although its numbers have tumbled they haven't fallen as badly as those of the song thrush. Both thrushes sing beautifully and the only description for both of them can be 'songbird'.

The long-tailed tit is another bird of a winter hedgerow; these are very distinctive and attractive birds in winter, moving as a family party along the hedgerows looking for food, all chattering away to one another. I think this picture of a little party of long-tailed tits is one of the best bird pictures that Gordon painted. It really does catch the mood and character perfectly. The good thing too is that numbers of long-tailed tits over the last twenty-five years have increased by 61 per cent. The reason is probably because, in addition to the hedgerow and the wood, the long-tailed tit frequents gardens more than it used to and there it gets a degree of protection as well as food.

Wrens too are found all along the hedgerows as well as in the farmyard and garden. Consequently the hedgerow really is the refuge of the songbird – its place in the wildlife cycle is extremely important.

One more summer bird of the hedgerow is the whitethroat, which is another of those birds whose numbers are thankfully increasing and shows a plus of 34 per cent. It has a lovely song, but it is also a bird that it will scold with a very harsh and rattling call if an intruder gets too near its nest or territory.

Two birds increasing in numbers, long-tailed tits (left) and the melodic wren (right).

The happy white throat on the sweeing bough
Swayed by the impulse of the gadding wind
That usher in the showers of april – now
Singeth right joyously and now reclined
Croucheth and clingeth to her moving seat
To keep her hold and till the wind for rest
Pauses she mutters inward melody
That seems her hearts rich thinkings to repeat
And when the branch is still her little breast
Swells out in raptures gushing symphonies
And then against her brown wing softly prest
The wind comes playing an enraptured guest
This way and that she swees – till gusts arise
More boisterous in their play – when off she flies
                                            John Clare

One reason for the whitethroat to scold could be the approach of a little owl. The little owl is also a bird of hedgerow, field and woodland. Originally introduced from North America, it has succeeded in not only becoming part of our countryside, but also more popular than many other introduced species. It will take young fledglings, but its main diet is insects and rodents and it is a most attractive and intelligent bird.

OPPOSITE: *The whitethroat – a good singer and a lover of wild scrubby places.*
RIGHT: *The little owl – an adopted immigrant.*

CHAPTER SEVEN

Woodland

Gordon enjoyed walking through woodland at any time of year; it didn't have to be a large wood, it could be just a spinney, or a copse or just a group of trees. As an artist it was shapes, colours, textures, scents, sounds and the wind blowing through the branches that appealed to him. In spring, there were flowers and the dawn chorus. In summer, birds were still singing with the leaves giving dappled, dancing light. In the autumn he always went down to Dorset to Powerstock, to see the rut of the fallow deer, and in winter he was attracted by early morning frost, the damp smell and feel of fallen leaves underfoot. Living here in Hertfordshire we are lucky, as we are not far from the beautiful woods of Ashridge owned by the National Trust. It was being so near to Ashridge, as well as several other little woods and copses, that gave Gordon the chance to do his appealing paintings of bluebells, woods and deer.

The bird that excited him every time he heard it, of course was the nightingale. It has such a wonderful song and the whole wood seems to echo and reverberate with almost a celebration of sound. Nightingales are quite difficult to see, but when you do manage to get a glimpse of them, they are very beautiful. It's a shame that their numbers, and consequently, their song, have declined by 42 per cent over the last twenty-five years.

When we were young we would hear the nightingale regularly but it has declined as lots of the little spinneys and copses have disappeared from the landscape. There are many big woods around of course and the nightingale hangs on; but its demise is a very sad loss for the English countryside. Several birds will sing after dusk, particularly where street lights are involved, but the nightingale sings loudest and longest. Some people think that

A woodland spring – bluebells flower and the nightingale sings.

any bird that sings after dark is a nightingale but they are usually quite wrong. John Clare made some very interesting observations about the nightingale:

I forgot to say in my last that the Nightingale sung as common by day as night and as often tho its a fact that is not generaly known your Londoners are very fond of talking about this bird and I believe fancy every bird they hear after sunset a Nightingale I remember when I was there last while walking with a friend in the fields of Shacklwell we saw a gentleman and lady listning very attentive by the side of a shrubbery and when we cam up we heard them lavishing praises on the beautiful song of the nightingale which happened to be a

LEFT: *The nightingale, lover of scrubby woods and tangles.*

RIGHT: *Woodpigeons like woods too.*

thrush but it did for them and they listend and repeated their praise with heart felt satisfaction while the bird seemed to know the grand distinction that its song had gaind for it and strove exultingly to keep up the deception by attempting a varied and more louder song the dews was ready to fall but the lady was heedless of the wet grass tho the setting sun as a traveller glad to rest was leaning his enlargd rim on the earth like a table of fire and lessening by degrees out of sight leaving night and a few gilt clouds behind him such is the ignorance of nature in large Citys that are nothing less then overgrown prisons that shut out the world and all its beautys

Gordon would very much have approved of this Clare quote because he felt very strongly that the countryside was being dominated more and more by urban politicians and incomers who simply do not understand the countryside and the way it works. They

regard it as some kind of theme park, and see traditional country people as unsophisticated peasants whose culture can be changed and swept away.

The pictures in this chapter show Gordon's love of both woodland and woodland birds.

Great trees and leaves, branches and clearings seem to give sound an added clarity in woodland and so the song of the nightingale seems to be more liquid and have more clarity inside a large wood than in a clump of brambles or a small copse. Similarly the clatter of pigeons is something that you associate with woodlands and in these pictures here you can almost smell the dampness and hear the pigeons as they are disturbed and fly off. Gordon was fond of both these pictures; he was fond of pigeon pie as well.

There are other sounds in woods as well, and the rook is a bird that needs high trees to build its nests in, before they are in leaf. Swaying rookeries and the call of rooks

are an essential part of woodland life. When the birds are on the ground searching for food they look elegant, like serious old gentlemen strutting around. Once in the air and at the nest, they are very sociable birds and very loyal. Although the nests look a complete jumble they are in fact skilfully made.

One of the problems linked to global warming is that if our fields become drier the rooks will find it very difficult to prod and probe around for worms, insects and seeds, and in some parts of the continent where rooks could be expected it is said that they are a rarity, because the soil is too hard and dry. If the sound of rooks in rookeries ever passes away, it will be a very sad day for the countryside.

John Clare was also fond of rooks:

The rooks begin to build and pleasant looks
The homestead elms now almost black with rooks
The birds at first for mastership will try
They fight for sticks and squabble as they flye
And if a stranger comes they soon invade
And pull his nest in pieces soon as made
The carrion crow and hawk dare never come
They dare to fight like armys round their home
The boughs will hardly bear their noisey guests
And storms will come and over turn the nests
They build above the reach of clauming crows
They climb and feel but cunning cuts them down
Others with reaching poles the nest destroys
While off and up they flye with deafening noise

The jay is another member of the crow family that lives in woodlands and indeed gardens. We occasionally see them here and they are extremely beautiful birds. People are divided as to whether they are good or bad. I suppose they do take eggs and fledglings if they find them, but they are particularly famous for taking acorns and beech nuts and in fact, so I am told, the second part of their scientific name *glandarius* actually means 'eating acorns and beech nuts'.

111

One good thing about the jay is that it lets out a raucous rattling call whenever strangers are about and so it makes a very good watchdog – or 'watchbird' – for the other birds of the woodland. It is extremely beautiful and some country people use the brilliant black and turquoise feathers of the jay in their hat bands. John Clare has written about this 'watchbird':

The jay set up his copple crown
And screamed to see a stranger
And swopt and hurried up and down
To warn the birds of danger
And magpies where the spinney was
Noised five and six together
While patiently the woodmans ass
Stood stretching round his tether

ABOVE: *The jay – lover of acorns.*
LEFT: *Rooks in the high tops of the rookery.*

The hammering of the great-spotted woodpecker is another woodland feature in the spring and as it hammers the sound seems to echo around the wood. The great-spotted woodpecker is now quite a common bird and it is really exciting the way it has recovered from its recent very low numbers. It is a beautiful bird of striking colour and it is another of the birds that has adapted to peanuts in people's gardens. It is a common sight for woodpeckers to bring their young into gardens to get easy food by swinging on nut holders. Consequently they will often leave their woodland homes to call into a garden with peanuts, rather like dropping into a snack bar or a roadside café. John Clare used to try unsuccessfully to steal its eggs:

There is a small woodpecker red and grey
That hides in woods and forrests far away
They run like creepers up and down the tree
And few can find them when they stand to see
They seldom fly away but run and climb
A man may stand and look for twenty time
And seldom see them once for half a day
Ive stood nor seen them till they flew away
Ive swarmed the grain and clumb with hook and pole
But scarce could get three fingers in the hole
They build on grains scarse thicker that ones legs
Ive found the nests but never got the eggs
But boys who wish to see what eggs they lay
Will climb the tree and saw the grain away

John Clare

Another startling sound in woodland at dusk is that of the 'roding' woodcock. It can hardly be called a songbird, but its territorial flight and its peculiar call is in its way very beautiful; in fact it almost sounds like an airborne frog. Gordon regarded the woodcock as one of our most beautiful birds with its feathers being a subtle blend of browns, duns and russets to match its surroundings of bracken, brown leaves and branches. He was intrigued too, by the folklore that has grown up surrounding the woodcock, particularly at the belief that woodcock can carry their young in flight. The debate has raged for generations. Some claim that the chicks accidentally get caught up in the feathers as the bird

The great-spotted woodpecker – lover of woods and garden peanuts.

114

ABOVE: *The woodcock – bird of woodland and folklore.*

RIGHT: *The willow tit – also known as the 'March Nightingale'.*

takes off, and others insist that the woodcock quite deliberately carries its young from place to place. Whatever is the truth of the matter it is an astonishing bird. It seems to be breeding more and more commonly throughout Britain and numbers swell with winter visitors once the weather turns cold in the autumn.

The next three birds unfortunately do not all have beautiful songs, but they are very attractive birds of woodland and as we were fortunate to find the pictures; I thought it was right to include them in the book.

The first is of the willow tit, which is the exception, as it can sing. It is a very attractive bird and for years the marsh tit and the willow tit were thought to be one and the same species. They are very difficult to tell apart; it would seem that the simplest way is finding their nests. The willow tit excavates its own nest hole, the marsh tit finds a natural hole or crack in which to build. The other simple way to differentiate between them,

116

according to one naturalist, is that the willow tit likes marshes and the marsh tit likes willows. That is an over-simplification – the willow tit likes damp woods with decaying trees including willow, birch and alder where it can make its nest. Like so many other birds it is in serious decline and numbers have fallen by 50 per cent. Unusually for the tit family, the willow tit has a very attractive song and some people have even mistaken it for a nightingale. John Clare confirms that the confusion has lasted for many generations:

> ... *I think I had the good luck today to hear the bird which you spoke of last March as singing early in spring and which you so apropriatly named the mock nightingale for some its notes are exactly similar I heard it singing in 'Open Wood' and was startled at first to think it was the nightingale and tryd to creep in to the thicket to see if I coud discover what bird it was but it seemd to be very shoy and got further from me as I approachd till I gave up the pursuit – I askd some Woodmen who were planting under wood at the time wether they know the bird and its song seemd to be very familiar to them they said it always came with the first fine*

LEFT: *The redpoll – top of Britain's league table for vanishing birds.*
RIGHT: *The delicate treecreeper – on the increase.*

days of spring and assured me it was the wood chat but they coud not agree with each
others opinion for another believd it to be the large black cap or black headed Titmouse so I
coud get nothing for fact but I shall keep a sharp look out when I hear it again …

In this poem, *March Nightingale*, Clare puts his confusion into verse – 'Blackcaps' used
here is another country name for willow tit.

Now sallow catkins once all downy white
Turn like the sunshine into golden light
The rocking clown leans oer the spinney rail
In admiration at the sunny sight
The while the Blackcap doth his ears assail
With such a rich and such an early song
He stops his own and thinks the nightingale
Hath of her monthly reckoning counted wrong
'Sweet jug jug jug' comes loud upon his ear
Those sounds that unto may by right belong
Yet on the awthorn scarce a leaf appears
How can it be – spell struck the wondering boy
Listens again – again the sound he hears
And mocks it in his song for very joy

The redpoll is another bird that loves woodland, particularly woodland containing alders,
birches and conifers as it is a great seed eater. Sadly its greatest claim to fame these days is
that it tops the league table in Britain's vanishing birds as it has declined by an alarming
92 per cent. It is a very beautiful little bird and Gordon's picture on page 118 captures
both the beauty and the character perfectly.

At least one of Gordon's birds of woodland is increasing and that is the treecreeper.
It has increased by 13 per cent and it is a bird that he found fascinating to watch. It is so
delicate and small and as it searches for food along the cracks of bark it blends almost
totally with the colours of the tree itself. It is a very pretty bird and has a number of
country names. In Yorkshire it is known as 'little woodpecker', while in Suffolk they call it
both 'bark creeper' and 'bark runner'. In Sussex, it is 'tree crawler' while in Somerset it is
'tree mouse'. I think treecreeper is the best name as it does seem to creep up the tree as it
searches for food.

The tawny owl – lover of the woodland night.

ABOVE: *Moonlight and hooting owls so often go together.*
LEFT: *A tawny owl above badgers: one of Gordon's last commissioned paintings.*

There is another bird too that has a variety of country names. In various parts it is called the 'hollering owl', the 'screech owl' and even the 'hill hooter'. It is the tawny owl or brown owl and its call goes with the darkness of the woodland night. Gordon often visited woods in the moonlight. In the painting with its clump of trees and moonlight, you can almost hear a tawny owl hooting. It is a beautiful sound and a beautiful feeling to be out in woodland with the moon shining bright and casting the shadows of branches and tree trunks. It is amazing what you can see in a wood at night, under a full moon. In Dorset Gordon loved watching the fallow deer in moonlight with his friend Dennis Furnell, and hearing that beautiful accompaniment of the tawny owl. Tawny numbers too have fallen by 33 per cent because of the great loss of spinneys, copses and the rough places where small mammals provide the owl's diet.

The picture of the owl above the badger links three of Gordon's loves in one picture – woodland, tawny owls and badgers. Badgers are not necessarily animals of woods – they will dig out a sett anywhere they consider suitable from dense bramble thicket to open field. Gordon spent many woodland dusks watching badgers and seeing their cubs play.

Foxes too can be seen anywhere, sleeping in a woodland glade, hunting a hedgerow or diving after voles in long grass. Gordon took a very common-sense view of foxes; he believed them to be beautiful, intelligent animals, but he disagreed with people who claim they do no damage to wildlife. He also disagreed with those who want to kill every single fox for the sake of a few pheasants. He believed that if there were too many foxes, their numbers should be reduced, if there were only a few foxes they should be left alone. He also believed that hunting was one of the best ways to both control and protect foxes because no huntsman wants fox extinction. It is a pity more people don't take his common-sense view.

So Gordon loved woodlands and the birds of woodland and I hope these pictures help to show that appreciation. In fact Gordon regarded it as one of the great honours of his life when the Woodland Trust planted 'Beningfield's Wood' in Dorset very close to Kingcombe, an area of which he was very fond. He went down to Dorset to help plant the first trees and I am glad to say that they are all growing well and in years to come the wood will be a long-lasting and living tribute to Gordon.

CHAPTER EIGHT

Wayside

The good thing about the traditional countryside is that surprising birds can be seen at any time. When Gordon was looking for something to paint, he would just wander through the countryside in the hope of seeing things of beauty and interest. He found the old farm tracks, driftways, ancient drove roads, sheep walks and footpaths attractive because they link old fields and old parishes with old woodland and wetland. Wandering over stiles with the birds singing on a summer day can only be described as a genuine pleasure. Once out of the range of traffic noise, the full splendour of the English countryside can be appreciated.

Along the stream, a turquoise flash can be seen as a kingfisher hurtles by. They are really beautiful birds, probably as far as colour goes, the most stunning birds in Britain. Their call is very high pitched and cannot be mistaken. We are very lucky because we regularly see kingfishers along the River Gade. In Dorset when Gordon was researching or retracing the steps of Hardy or his characters, he would often see kingfishers along those lovely little Dorset streams. Because of his regard for Dorset, the Countryside Restoration Trust hopes to

Wayside – with surprises around every corner.

125

buy a farm in Gordon's memory and one day there could be both a Beningfield Wood and a Beningfield Farm, which is a most exciting thought.

Although throughout the book I have been referring to John Clare; for the kingfisher I have to quote WH Davies's famous poem. I suppose Davies was rather like Clare as although he had no special education, he lived a remarkable life; his most famous book was *The Autobiography of a Super-Tramp*. Gordon admired his poetry and his best-known poem, *Leisure*, starts:

> *What is this life if, full of care,*
> *We have no time to stand and stare …*

His wonderful descriptive poem, *The Kingfisher*, was also once learnt by every school student.

G. Beningfield.

It was the Rainbow gave thee birth,
And left thee all her lovely hues;
And, as her Mother's name was Tears,
So runs it in my blood to choose
For haunts the lonely pools, and keep
In company with trees that weep.

Go you and, with such glorious hues,
Live with proud Peacocks in green parks;
On lawns as smooth as shining glass,
Let every feather show its marks;
Get thee on boughs and clap thy wings
Before the windows of proud kings.

Nay, lovely Bird, thou art not vain;
Thou hast no proud, ambitious mind;
I also love a quiet place
That's green, away from all mankind;
A lonely pool, and let a tree
Sigh with her bosom over me.

The kestrel is another bird of wayside. It isn't a songbird, but it is a bird that once inhabited every single parish in the country, and of course one of its country names, 'windhover' describes exactly how it hangs in the air, hovering, as it searches for its prey, either small mammals, birds or insects. It is a beautiful bird, but sadly its numbers have declined by 24 per cent.

In Dorset, whilst wandering, it was even possible to see a peregrine falcon, a wonderful bird which has complete mastery of the air. Its shape, speed and cry really bring up mental images of wild places. After the terrible knocks it took because of DDT, when it edged close to extinction in Britain, it is good to have this magnificent bird back again.

Sadly one other bird that has not yet been saved from approaching extinction in Britain is the snipe – numbers have tumbled by 90 per cent. Again this is one of Gordon's early pictures but it has a definite charm. It would have been wonderful for him to have

The kestrel or 'windhover' – it now finds motorway verges more attractive than many fields.

ABOVE: *An early picture of a snipe.*
LEFT: *The peregrine now totally recovered after being on the brink of British extinction.*

painted a modern water meadow scene with the snipe drumming high above. 'Drumming' is the amazing sound that the snipe makes when it is displaying. The drumming is caused by the snipe diving during its display flight; the vibrating humming sound is produced by the air rushing through the widely spread tail feathers.

The reasons for the demise of the snipe are many, and it really is a tragedy. Along the Gade in winter, snipe would spring up into the air and it was a common sight wherever there was damp grass, a ditch or stream. Sadly again, it is loss of habitat due to the industrialisation of farming, the draining of wet meadows and marshland, and also the increased stocking rates of cattle and sheep that have all contributed to the decline. Once when farming was more natural and the treatment of animals was better, then the snipe could nest at the base of a clump of reeds or a tuft of grass, and the likelihood of the eggs being trampled was small. Now because of the sheer numbers of animals, the snipe's eggs will often be trampled.

In some places it has been reported that sparrowhawks specialise in catching snipe in marshy areas; they fly low and slow over the area using almost the same techniques as hen harriers to flush the birds out, and dive on them just as they leave the ground. It can only be hoped that common sense soon prevails over the drainage of land and the way we treat animals, so that water, space, beautiful meadows and quiet marshy places return. These might then might bring the snipe back into our everyday lives. John Clare's poem, *To the Snipe*, is really one of his best:

BENINGFIELD'S VANISHING SONGBIRDS

Lover of swamps
The quagmire over grown
With hassock tufts of sedge – where fear encamps
Around thy home alone

The trembling grass
Quakes from the human foot
Nor hears the weight of man to let him pass
Where thou alone and mute

Sittest at rest
In safety neath the clump
Of high flag forrest that thy hants invest
Or some old sallow stump

Thriving on seams
That tiney islands swell
Just hilling from the mud and rancid streams
Suiting they nature well

For here thy bill
Suited by wisdom good
Of rude unseemly length doth delve and drill
The gelid mass for food

And here may hap
When summer suns hath drest
The mores rude desolate spungy lap
May hide they mystic nest

Mystic indeed
For isles that ocean made
Are scarcely more secure for birds to breed
Than this flag hidden lake…

The stonechat, another lover of gorse.

Another bird that Gordon saw regularly in Dorset is the stonechat. The stonechat, like the linnet on heathland, loves gorse and it is almost true to say that wherever there are gorse bushes near the coast, a stonechat will not be far away. The male is a very attractive little bird with a dark head and white collar. The female is attractive too, but not quite so gaudy as the male.

The Dartford warbler was one of Gordon's favourite birds, as this is a real bird of Dorset heathland and another lover of gorse. At one time it was limited to the heaths of Hampshire, Dorset and Surrey, and after the very cold winter of 1962–63 naturalists, including Gordon, were alarmed as numbers fell to just ten pairs. Because the Dartford warbler depends so much on insects, cold winters have a devastating effect on it and 1962–63 was certainly almost a Dartford warbler tragedy. Fortunately since then the little bird has not only recovered, it has also quite literally spread its wings and it can now be found in Avon, Berkshire, Norfolk and Suffolk. It is most attractive and if you see a Dartford warbler it is one of those little birds that can be mistaken for no other species. Looking at the Dartford warbler would take Gordon back to the Hardy stories that he loved; *Tess of the D'Urbervilles*, *Jude the Obscure* and *The Woodlanders*. It was one of Gordon's great pleasures that he got to know Gertrude Bugler who actually played Tess for Thomas Hardy; the story was that when she was a young girl, Hardy was infatuated by her. Certainly Gordon could understand that, because even at a very great age she still had a wonderful happy face and beautiful eyes.

It is appropriate that I finish this chapter with a bird of heathland, of Dorset, and of moonlit summer nights. It is the bird that Gordon hoped to hear and see in Hardy country. The nightjar is a truly astonishing bird. It sits tight and close along branches, not across them and its camouflage and finely mottled plumage makes it very difficult to see. It nests on the ground and amongst the bracken; it is almost impossible to find the bird or its nest without expert help. It is one of nature's master-pieces. It is also a bird that as the sun sets it begins to call, and the males make an incredible *churring* noise. If you throw a white handkerchief into the air they will even swoop at it, presumably mistaking it for an intruder. They hawk the heathland for moths and insects, and when they are hunting they can open their mouths to an incredible

ABOVE: *The mysterious nightjar.*
LEFT: *The Dartford warbler, another bird of Dorset heathland.*

135

ABOVE: *Eggardon Hill in moonlight.*

size. Like many other birds the nightjar was in steep decline, but fortunately the drop has been halted and with all the work to restore heathland and wilderness the nightjar is actually making a comeback. Gordon was very happy about this because it is such a remarkable bird. Of course, John Clare knew of it and wrote:

> *… The Fern Owl or Goat sucker or Night jar or night hawk while several more or's might be added no doubt to fresh names is a curious bird they are found about us in summer on a wild heath calld Emmingsales and I believe that is the only spot which they visit they make an odd noise in the evening beginning at dewfall and continuing it at intervals all night it is a beautifull object in Poetic Nature – from that peculiarity alone one cannot pass over a wild heath in a summer evening without being stopt to listen and admire its novel and pleasing noise it is a trembling sort of crooing sound which may be nearly imitated by making a crooing noise and at the same time patting the finger before the mouth to break the sound like stopping a hole in the German flute to quaver a double sound on one note this noise is generally made as it descends from a*

bush or tree for its prey it is said to feed on insects that breed on the fox fern whense it name it is beautiful mottld bird variously shadowd with the colors of black and brown it appears of the hawk tribe

The picture of Eggardon Hill, sums up Gordon's love of the countryside and it reminds me of the nights that he would go out hoping to hear the nightingale, the nightjar or rutting deer at the right season.

And lastly the signpost through the countryside. This is the real wayside; the heart of the countryside. I hope these paintings not only help people to see the beauty of our wildlife, but also inspire them to look after it and cherish it.

Backword

Although much of the message of this book is a warning, full of gloom and doom, Gordon did see hope. He believed that the countryside could be restored and the birds, butterflies, flowers and animals that he loved so much could be encouraged back into the wild. He was convinced that restoration was the conservation of the future and that countryside, and countrywide restoration could be achieved.

He totally endorsed the work of Butterfly Conservation, The Royal Society for the Protection of Birds (RSPB), the Wildlife Trusts, the Game Conservancy and the Woodland Trust. He agreed that rare and special species should be protected and so wildlife reserves and areas with built in, legal protection, were important. But he was sure that long-term conservation would only be successful if it occurred in the general countryside, on farmland, commonland and land owned by the government, local authorities and institutions. Why should people have to get into a car and travel miles to see a barn owl, a bee orchid or signs of otters, in a special 'nature reserve', when once they could be seen in virtually every parish in the country?

To Gordon, things were simple. If wildlife had been damaged through habitat destruction and pesticide use – the solution was easy – restore the lost habitat and use less chemicals.

Similarly it was obvious to him that too many predators could damage vulnerable species of bird and animal. Again he took a practical, common-sense approach – if there were too many predators – foxes, crows or magpies – control them – not exterminate them. If there were too few predators – leave them alone. In the 'predator debate' he could never understand why some species, such as deer, could be shot to protect rare plants. But birds of prey could

A pair of bullfinches – often a target of sparrowhawks.

never be managed even if they were eating rare birds. The two most obvious examples being the long-established impact of the now common sparrowhawk on the disappearing bullfinch, and the effect of hen harriers on a range of rapidly declining moorland birds.

In believing that conservation and farming go hand-in-hand, Gordon was well ahead of his time. It was way back in 1980 that he telephoned me and asked me to go to the RSPB's headquarters with him. The new Wildlife and Countryside Act was to be discussed in Parliament and he wanted the RSPB, with the power of its large membership behind it, to put pressure on the politicians to protect the whole countryside and not just special areas.

The then Director of the RSPB did not know what had hit him. Gordon was asking him to support the legal protection of hedgerows, old grass meadows and water meadows on ordinary farmland – the general countryside. Conservation on such a scale was, at that time, too much for the RSPB to comprehend. Ian Prestt made it clear that the conservationists of the day supported reserves and Sites of Special Scientific Interest – 'island conservation'. Gordon became so frustrated that he banged his fist down on the table, much to the surprise of Ian Prestt. From his reaction it seemed that the Director was more used to plaudits, admiration, and touched forelocks from those who visited the inner sanctum of the RSPB. We were eventually shown the door with Gordon's message being way beyond the RSPB's vision and understanding at that time.

Still, the destruction of wildlife continued at an alarming speed: wildflowers disappeared, woodlands and hedgerows were bulldozed away, water meadows were drained and the farmland bird population crashed. Government stooges and advisers defended this politically inspired vandalism by saying food production was the same as car production and so farming should get no special conditions or subsidies. Such environmental illiteracy overlooks the fact that barn owls, bee orchids and otters do not live in car factories – they do live in the countryside. Consequently the whole ethos of farming should be based not simply on efficiency, profit, and competitiveness, but on responsibility and sustainability. How can you put a price, or an efficiency rating, on a skylark or a bullfinch?

So in 1993, with no money, no members and no idea how to run a charity, we launched the Countryside Restoration Trust. Sir Laurens van der Post was the other great figure of encouragement and support in this totally blind venture. A financial adviser advised us not to go ahead, saying that we would attract little interest and raise two thousand pounds if we were lucky. Gordon and Laurens both agreed that we should ignore

A song thrush eating an apple.

Gordon's last painting, intended for this book – an unfinished song thrush.

this advice and launch the CRT. Since then we have raised nearly two million pounds, we have two farms, (hopefully three by the time this book is published), over 700 acres and 5000 members.

Our first purchase of twenty acres, next to a tributary of the River Cam, has grown to over 350 acres. Lark Rise Farm has been incredible. It has shown that everything Gordon said in 1980 was true and still is. An almost wildlife-dead, over-intensive Cambridgeshire prairie has been restored to life, while at the same time it is producing quality food at a profit. Using and tweaking techniques pioneered by the Game Conservancy for pheasants and partridges, we have used grass margins, beetle banks and wildlife strips. We have planted a wood, a spinney and miles of hedgerow. In addition using the prescription of that great conservation visionary, Miriam Rothschild, we have restored traditional hay meadows along the small brook; while Tim Scott our tenant farmer, has been farming in a way that is acceptable both to farmers and conservationists alike.

As a result Lark Rise Farm is already teeming with wildlife. It is thought that we have the highest density of skylarks in East Anglia and we have a host of other farmland birds that elsewhere are considered to be at risk. We have willow warblers, corn buntings, meadow pippits, reed buntings, English partridges, house sparrows, yellow hammers, yellow wagtails and of course every other bush seems to have a linnet in-it. In addition we have brown argus butterflies, grass snakes, otters, harvest mice and the brown hare population is back to where it was in the 1950s. The RSPB has changed course too and is now working hard at improving the general countryside and its head man, Graham Wynne, has made several visits to Lark Rise Farm; indeed the RSPB has now bought its own farm and we have been pleased by their broadened horizons. Before Gordon's last illness, and brave fight, he saw the birds, butterflies and wildflowers returning to Lark Rise Farm and he could see his vision for the general countryside becoming a reality in one part of Cambridgeshire.

I will always remember 4 May 1998. It was the day after my birthday; the sun was warm bringing out the first orange tip butterfly of the year and the apple blossom in my garden was at its peak. On the CRT's land a thousand cowslips bloomed, and above, larks sang. There was fusion of scents, sounds and visual beauty; it was the art of nature. Such a day required painting; a painting that was quintessentially English. There was only one man who could have caught the mood to perfection – but tragically that was the day Gordon Beningfield died. A wreath made entirely from cowslips, picked on Lark Rise Farm, was placed on his grave. A song thrush sang – an unfinished painting of a song thrush was the last work of a courageous, gifted and good man. His family, his friends and the countryside still miss him.

ROBIN PAGE

Gordon Beningfield supported a number of important conservation and countryside organisations:

BUTTERFLY CONSERVATION,
PO Box 222, Dedham, Colchester, Essex CO7 6EY

THE COUNTRYSIDE ALLIANCE,
The Old Town Hall, 367 Kennington Road, London SE11 4PT

THE COUNTRYSIDE RESTORATION TRUST,
Barton, Cambridgeshire CB3 7AG

THE DORSET WILDLIFE TRUST,
Brooklands Farm, Forston, Dorchester, Dorset DT2 7AA

THE GAME CONSERVANCY TRUST,
Burgate Manor, Fordingbridge, Hampshire SP6 1EF

THE HERTFORDSHIRE AND MIDDLESEX WILDLIFE TRUST,
Grebe House, St Michael's Street, St Albans, Hertfordshire AL3 4SN

THE KINGCOMBE TRUST,
The Kingcombe Centre, Toller Porcorum, Dorchester, Dorset DT2 0EQ

THE NATIONAL TRUST,
36 Queen Anne's Gate, London SW1H 9AS

THE ROYAL SOCIETY FOR THE PROTECTION OF BIRDS,
The Lodge, Sandy, Bedfordshire SG19 2DL

THE WOODLAND TRUST,
Autumn Park, Dysart Road, Grantham, Lincolnshire NG31 6LL